The Ultimate Self-Teaching Method! — Level One

Play Mandolin Today!®

A Complete Guide to the Basics

by Douglas Baldwin

To access audio visit:
www.halleonard.com/mylibrary

Enter Code
1271-0755-1178-5582

All music tracks performed, recorded, and produced by
Douglas Baldwin at Coyote Music, 1 Flowerfield, St. James, NY

ISBN 978-1-4234-2142-9

Copyright © 2010 by HAL LEONARD LLC
International Copyright Secured All Rights Reserved

No part of this publication may be reproduced in any form or by
any means without the prior written permission of the Publisher.

Visit Hal Leonard Online at
www.halleonard.com

Contact us:
Hal Leonard
7777 West Bluemound Road
Milwaukee, WI 53213
Email: info@halleonard.com

In Europe, contact:
Hal Leonard Europe Limited
42 Wigmore Street
Marylebone, London, W1U 2RN
Email: info@halleonardeurope.com

In Australia, contact:
Hal Leonard Australia Pty. Ltd.
4 Lentara Court
Cheltenham, Victoria, 3192 Australia
Email: info@halleonard.com.au

Introduction

Track 1

Welcome to *Play Mandolin Today!*—the series designed to prepare you for any style of mandolin playing, from country to bluegrass to old-time—even rock and blues! Whatever your tastes in music, *Play Mandolin Today!* will give you the start you need.

About the Audio

It's easy and fun to play the mandolin, and the accompanying audio will make your learning even more enjoyable, as we take you step by step through each lesson and play many of the examples with a full band. Much like real lessons, the best way to learn the material is to read and practice a while on your own, then listen to the "teacher" on the audio. With *Play Mandolin Today!*, you can learn at your own pace. If there is ever something that you don't quite understand the first time through, go back to the audio and listen again. Every music example in the book has been given a track number, so when you want to practice a song again, you can find it right away.

Contents

Lesson 1—The Basics 3

Lesson 2—The First String: E 8

Lesson 3—The Second String: A 11

Lesson 4—The Third String: D 16

Lesson 5—The Fourth String: G 21

Lesson 6—Chords 30

Lesson 7—The Major Scale 38

Lesson 8—Minor Scales & Movable Chords 43

Lesson 1: The Basics

Parts of the Mandolin

The mandolin is a great instrument—it has a bright, commanding sound, and it's small and easy to carry. Mandolins come in many shapes, but all mandolins have the same basic parts in common, as shown in the diagram to the right. Mandolins have eight strings, grouped in four pairs. Each pair of strings is called a *course*, and each course is played as if it is a single string. So the mandolin is twice as easy to play as it looks!

Be sure your mandolin is in good playing condition. If you have any doubts about its playability, take it to a reputable music repair shop.

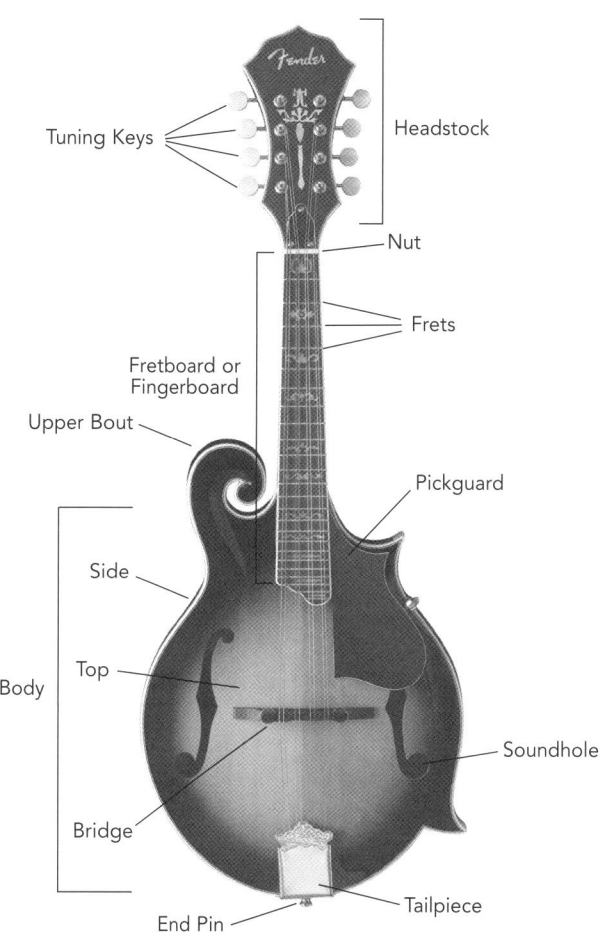

Track 2

How to Hold Your Mandolin

Because the mandolin is so small, it's a good idea to use an adjustable strap when you play. One end of the strap should attach to the strap pin at the end of the mandolin's body near the *tailpiece*, and the other end should attach to the strap pin near the neck. If you don't have a strap pin near the neck, you may attach the strap around the **upper bout** of the body. Adjust the strap so that the body of the mandolin is just below your rib cage and the neck is high enough to reach without bending your wrist. Keep the mandolin in place with the forearm of your picking hand. Whether you're standing or sitting, keep both hands free to play the strings.

Your Right and Left Hands

You'll be playing your mandolin by picking the strings with a pick held in your right hand. Most players hold the pick between the thumb and first finger.

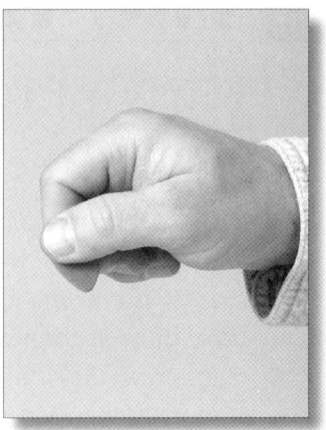

Bring your arm up so that the pick is parallel to the strings and pick with your wrist.

It's the job of your left hand to press the strings down to make different notes. Most of the time, your thumb should be behind the neck. With this position, your hand should be able to reach a distance of at least six frets.

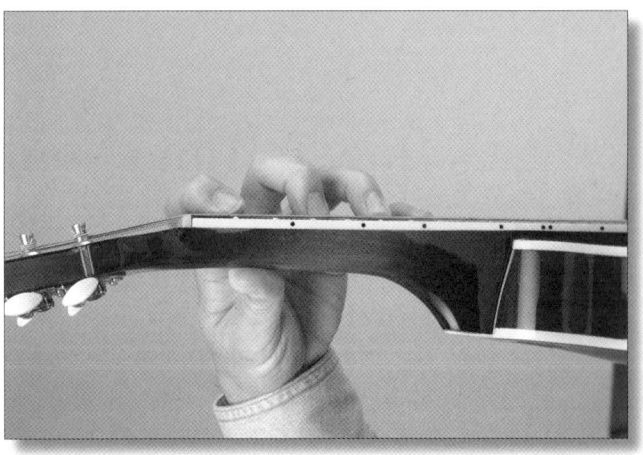

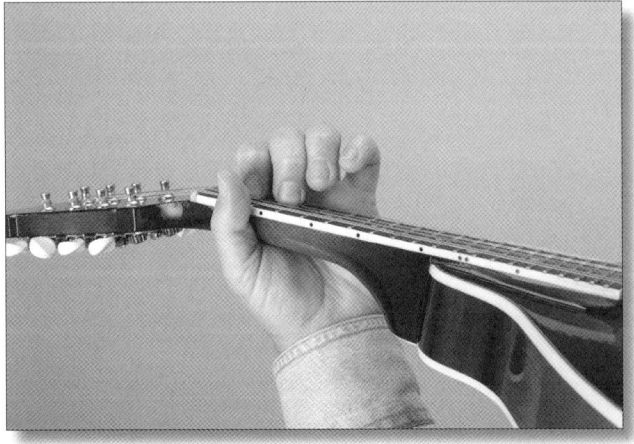

Sometimes, when your hand doesn't have to reach too far, you can wrap your thumb around the neck. Throughout this book and on the audio, I'll remind you where your thumb should be.

Playing Is Easy

If you haven't already, try picking the different pairs, or courses, of strings on your mandolin. Have you noticed that some sound higher and some sound lower? Each course has a different pitch. **Pitch** is the highness or lowness of a sound. On the mandolin, the string courses are numbered 1 through 4, from the highest-sounding strings (the thinnest) to the lowest (the thickest).

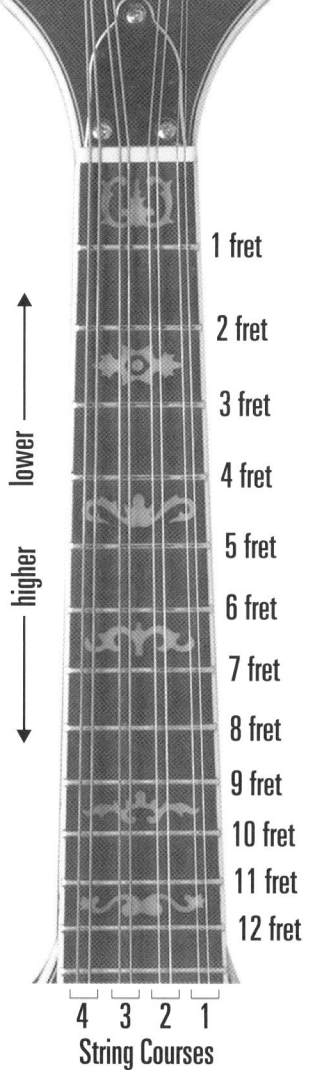

You get different pitches from each string course by pressing them down with your left hand so that they touch the metal frets. (You'll find that it's easy to press down both of the strings that make up a course, and it's almost impossible to press just one string at a time.) Fretting higher up the neck (closer to the body) produces sounds of a higher pitch; fretting lower (closer to the headstock) produces sounds of a lower pitch. As you can see on the diagram to the left, the frets of the mandolin are also numbered, from low (near the headstock) to high (near the body).

For your convenience, the fingers of your left hand will also be numbered in this book:

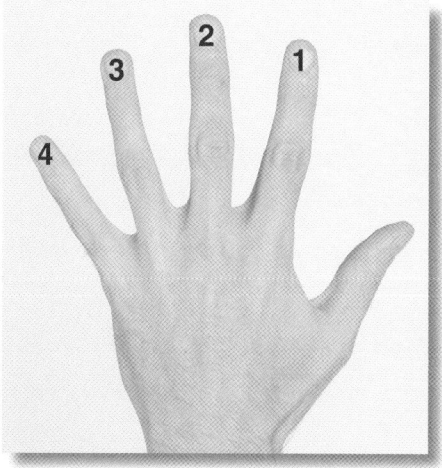

Track 3

Tuning Up

If you loosen a string by turning its **tuning key**, the pitch will become lower; if you tighten the string, the pitch will become higher. When two pitches sound exactly the same, they are said to be in **unison**, or **in tune**. The courses of the mandolin are tuned in unisons. There are many ways to tune the four courses of the mandolin: an electronic tuner, a piano, a pitch pipe, or a tuning fork—you can even tune your mandolin purely to itself. For now, however, listen to the audio to help you tune your instrument. The four open courses of the mandolin should be tuned to these pitches:

4 3 2 1
G–D–A–E
low ⟷ high

5

Here are a few tips to help you get started:

- Whether tightening or loosening a string, turn the tuning peg slowly so that you can concentrate on the change in pitch.

- Although you will usually pick both strings of a course when you play, pick just one string of a course at a time when you tune. You can mute the string you are not trying to tune with the tip of your thumb or finger.

- Instead of tuning a string *down* to pitch, tune it *up*. Tuning up allows you to stretch the string into place, which will help it stay in tune longer. So, if you begin with a string that is too high in pitch, tune it down below your target pitch first, then bring it back up to the target pitch.

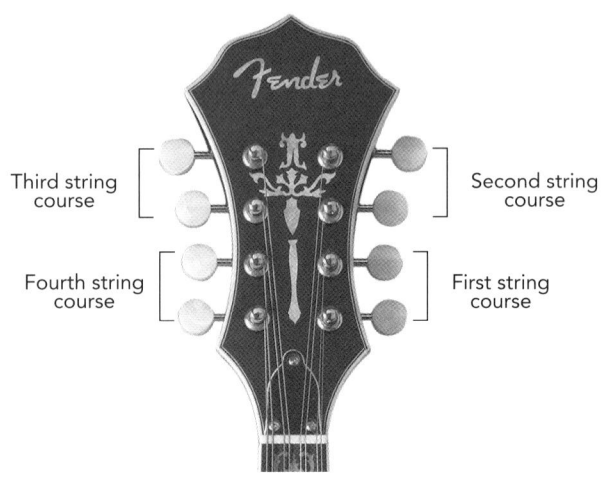

Another Way to Tune Your Mandolin

This is a great way to check your tuning or, if you don't have a pitch source like the accompanying audio, to tune your mandolin to itself.

1. Tune the 4th-string course G to a piano, a pitch pipe, an electronic tuner, or the accompanying audio. If none of these are available, approximate G the best you can. Be sure that both strings of the course are tuned in unison.

2. Press the 4th-string course at the seventh fret. This is the note D. Tune the open 3rd-string course to this pitch.

3. Press the 3rd-string course at the seventh fret. This is the note A. Tune the open 2nd-string course to this pitch.

4. Press the 2nd string course at the seventh fret. This is the note E. Tune the open 1st-string course to this pitch.

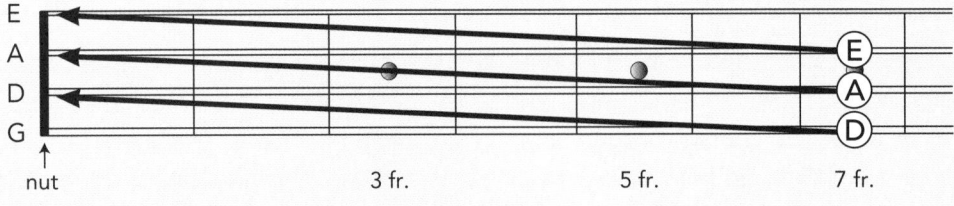

Note: From this point on, instead of referring to courses, we'll simply refer to strings. So, instead of saying "the 3rd-string course," we'll simply say "the 3rd string."

How to Read Music

Musical sounds are indicated by symbols called *notes*. Notes come in all shapes and sizes, but every note has two important components: *pitch* and *rhythm*.

Pitch

Pitch (the highness or lowness of a note) is indicated by the placement of the note on a *staff*, a set of five lines and four spaces.

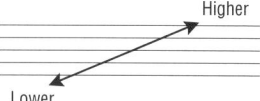

To name the notes on the staff, we use the first seven letters of the alphabet: **A–B–C–D–E–F–G**. Adding a *treble clef* assigns a particular note name to each line and space on the staff, centered on the pitch G, the second line from the bottom. The names of the lines, starting with the lowest, are E–G–B–D–F. The names of the spaces are F–A–C–E. Here are some easy ways to remember the names of the notes on the lines and spaces of the staff.

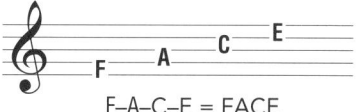

F–A–C–E = FACE

Because the mandolin uses notes both above and below the range of the staff, we use *ledger lines* to extend the staff's range.

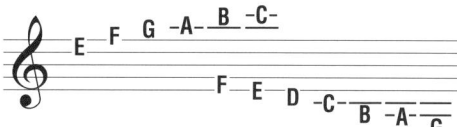

Rhythm

Rhythm refers to how long, or for how many beats, a note lasts. This is indicated with the following symbols:

Whole note (four beats)   Half note (two beats)   Quarter note (one beat)

To help you keep track of the beats in a piece of music, the staff is divided into *measures* (or "bars"). A *time signature* (or "meter") at the beginning of the staff indicates how many beats you can expect to find in each measure.

4/4 is perhaps the most common time signature. The top number (4) tells you how many beats there are in each measure; the bottom number (4) tells you what type of note value receives one beat. In 4/4 time, there are 4 beats in each measure, and a quarter note receives one beat.

7

Lesson 2: The First String: E

Track 4

The first four notes we'll learn on the mandolin are all found on the E string.

E

■ Your first note, E, is an open-string note. There's nothing to press down—simply strike the open 1st string with your pick.

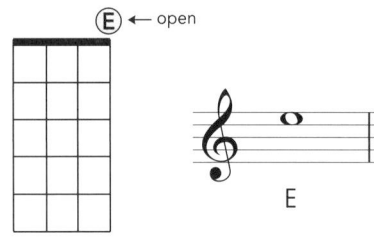

F

▶ Notice that your finger belongs directly behind each fret. If you place it on top of the fret or too far behind the fret, you'll have difficulty getting a full, clear sound.

■ For the next note, F, press your first finger on the 1st string directly behind the first fret and strike the string with your pick.

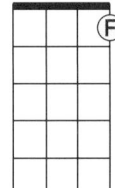

G

▶ Notice that, although you use your first finger for F and your second finger for G, you skip a fret between the notes.

■ For the note G, press your second finger on the 1st string directly behind the third fret and strike the string with your pick.

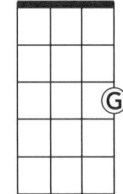

A

■ For the note A, press your fourth finger on the 1st string directly behind the fifth fret and strike the string with your pick.

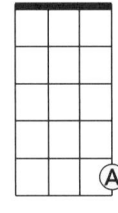
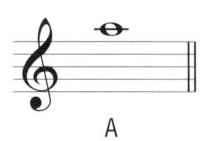

Learn to recognize these notes both on the fretboard and on the staff. Then, when you're comfortable playing the notes individually, try the song "E–F–G–A" on the next page. Speak the note names aloud as you play (e.g., "E, F, G, A...").

8

Track 5

E–F–G–A

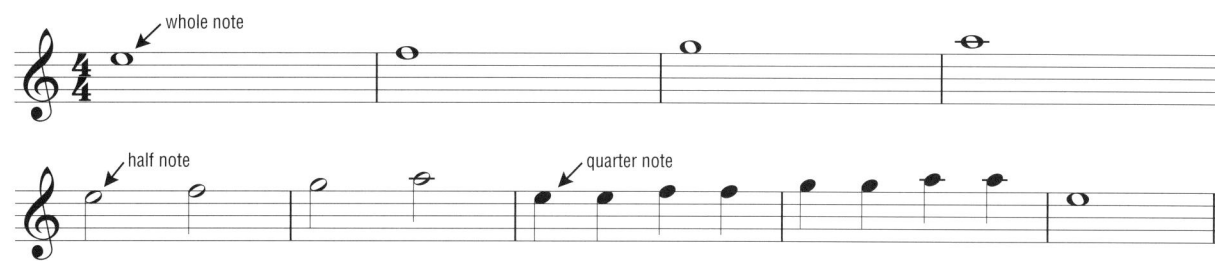

Of course, the best way to really learn these notes is to use them in some tunes—so let's do it. Start slowly with the following melodies and concentrate on keeping your tempo nice and even. Practice these several times on your own before you try playing along with the audio.

Track 6

Up and Down the Mountain

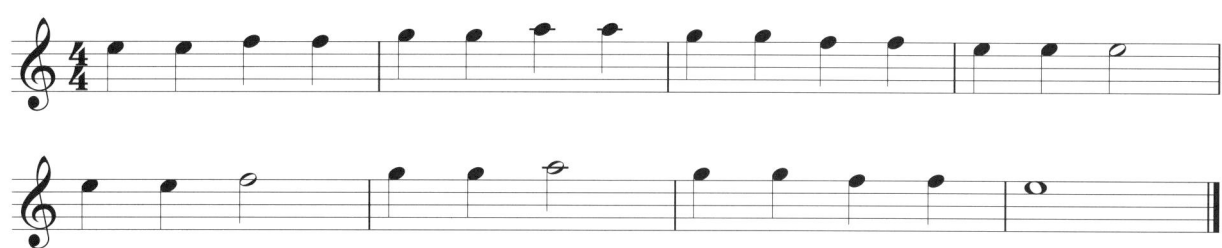

Keeping Time

Having trouble keeping a steady rhythm? Try *tapping* and *counting* along with each song. Use either foot to tap. Each time your foot comes down marks one beat. In 4/4 time, tap your foot evenly and count "one, two, three, four" for each measure. The first beat of each measure should be accented slightly—this is indicated by the symbol ">."

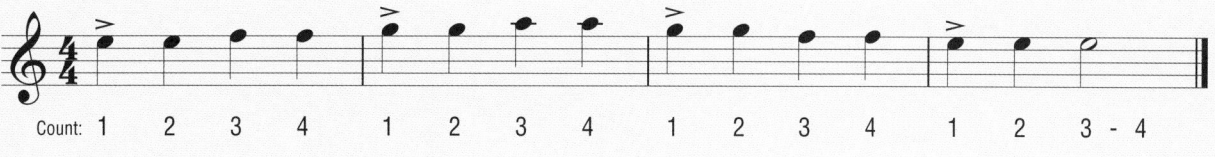

Track 7

Ski Song

▶ If you like, read through each song *without* your mandolin at first. Tap the beat with your foot, count out loud, and *clap* through the rhythms.

Skipping Song

Even though you don't actually use your left hand to fret the open E string, keep that hand on the mandolin in "ready position," with your thumb on the back of the neck. This will allow you to fret the other notes that much more quickly.

New Country

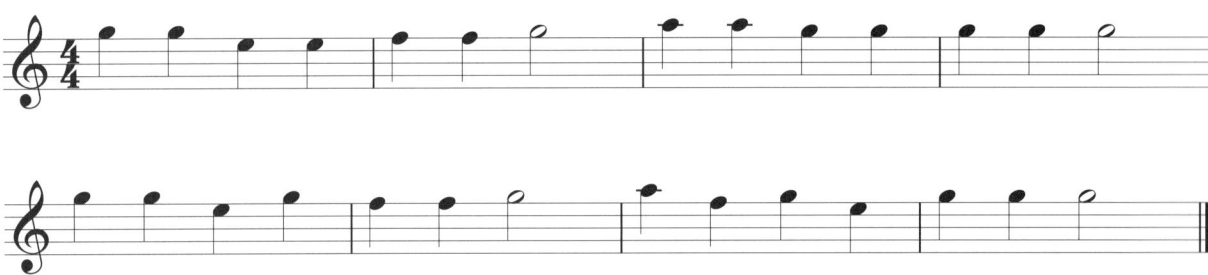

Lonesome Road

▶ Try to keep your eyes on the page instead of on your mandolin.

Picking with Downstrokes

Remember, you should be striking the strings with a downward motion of your pick. This is called a **downstroke** and is indicated with the "⊓" symbol.

Strive for efficiency and relaxation in your right-hand picking motion. It doesn't take much movement to get a good, solid downstroke.

Lesson 3: The Second String: A

Track 11

Your next four notes are all played on the 2nd string, A. You might want to check your tuning on that string before going any further.

A

▶ Notice that we now have two notes with the name "A." The open string is low in pitch, while the note you just learned on the E string, fifth fret is high in pitch.

■ To play the note A, just pick the open 2nd string.

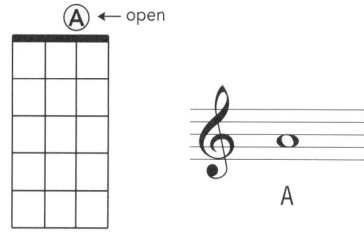

B

▶ Notice that the note B is on the second fret—not the first!

■ For the next note, B, press your first finger on the 2nd string directly behind the second fret and strike the string with your pick.

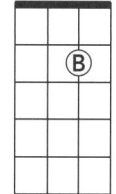 

C

■ For the note C, press your second finger on the 2nd string directly behind the third fret.

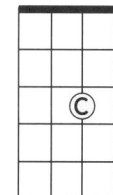 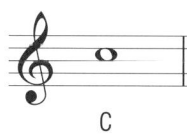

D

■ For the note D, press your fourth finger on the 2nd string directly behind the fifth fret.

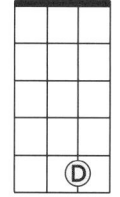 

Practice these next exercises several times, slow and easy. Then play them along with the audio. Again, say the note names out loud as you play.

A–B–C–D

It's quite a challenge to keep track of the notes on both the E and A strings. Let's play some more songs on the A string, then we'll mix these new notes in with the ones we've already learned.

Big Mountain

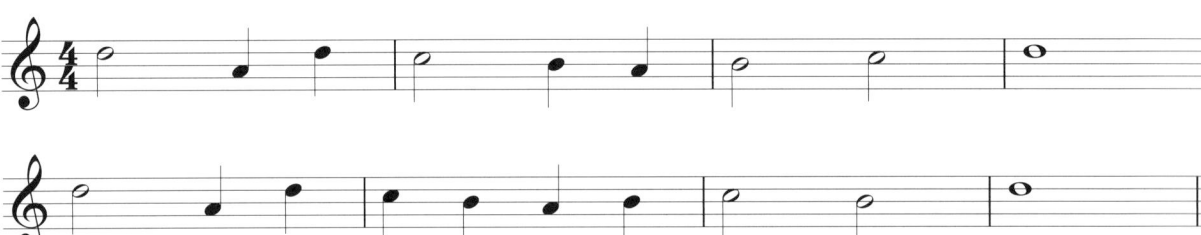

Etude de la Sol

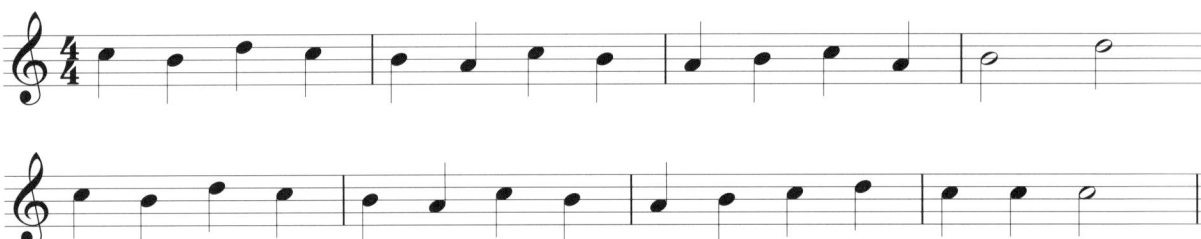

Now it's time to get back to the E string and add it to the new notes we've learned. You might want to review the notes from Lesson 2 before you go on.

All Mixed Up

▶ Remember, your first finger belongs on the first fret for the note F and on the second fret for the note B.

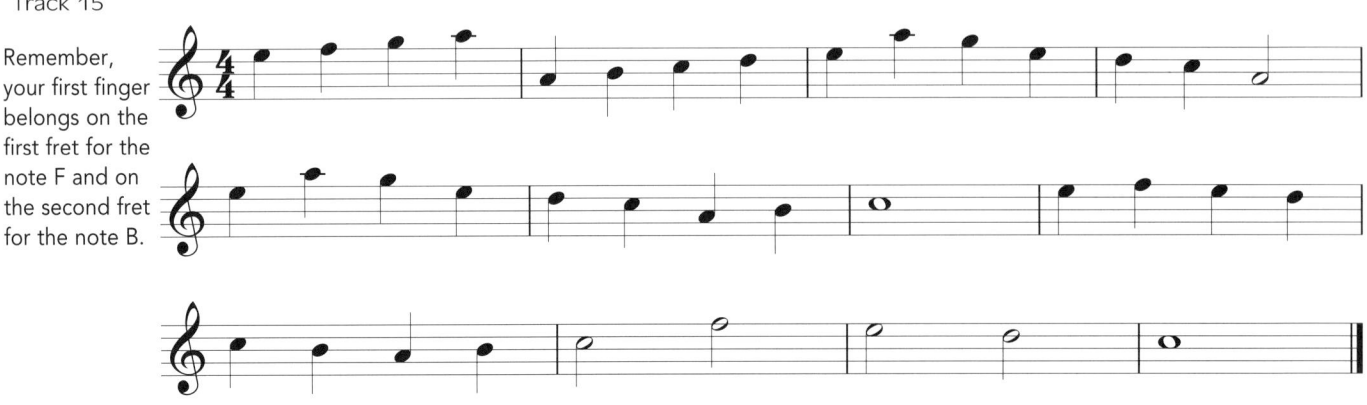

Track 16

Everything from A to A

Track 17

Introducing Rests

In addition to notes, songs often contain silences, or **rests**—beats in which you play nothing at all. A rest is a musical pause. Rests are like notes in that they have their own rhythmic values, instructing you how long (how many beats) to pause:

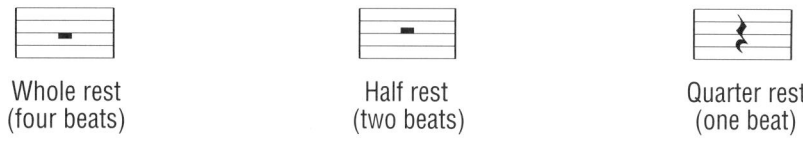

A rest really means quiet—not just "don't play." Your mandolin should stop ringing during a rest. To do this, try the following:

After an open-string note, like E or A, touch the string lightly with your left-hand fingers. After a fretted note, like F or B, relax your left-hand finger just enough so that the string stops ringing.

Try tapping and counting while playing this exercise.

Track 18

All the Rest

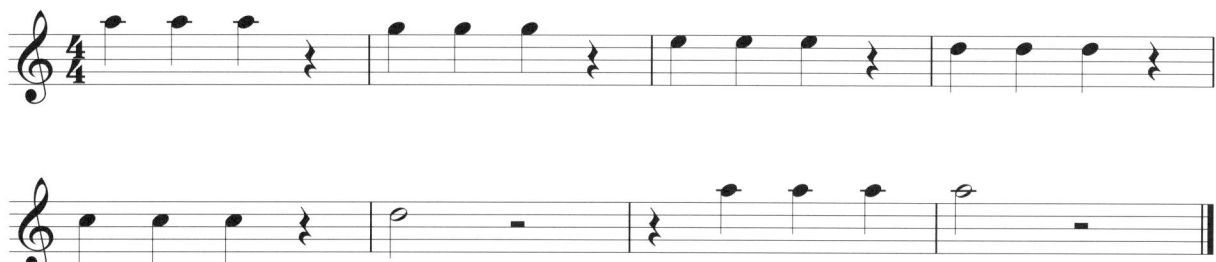

Track 19

Rest Assured

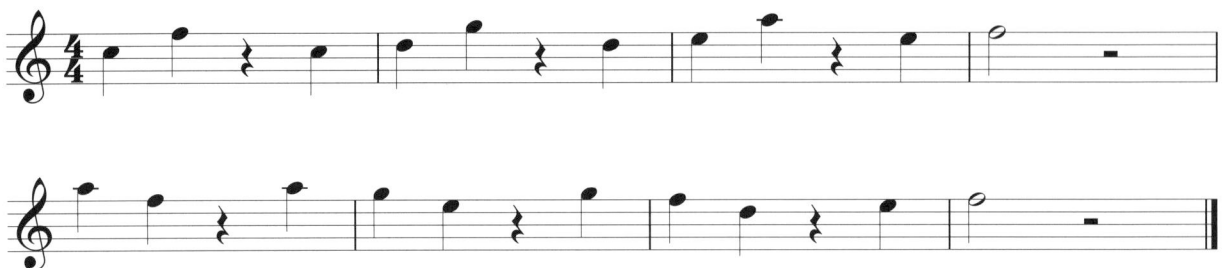

Introducing the Pickup

Instead of starting a song with a rest, a ***pickup measure*** is sometimes used. In a pickup, any opening rests are simply deleted.

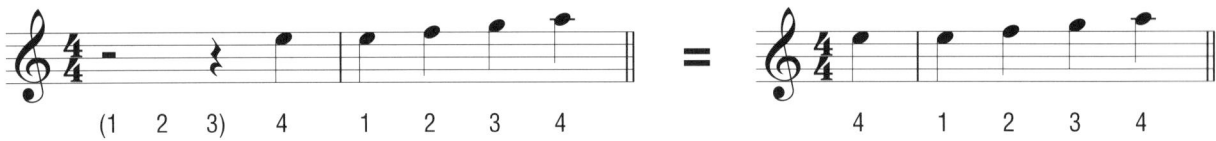

Usually, if a pickup has two or more beats, you'll want to count one full measure, then the beats before the pickup notes. If a pickup has only one beat, you count "1, 2, 3" and start playing on beat 4.

Track 20

When the Saints Go Marching In

▶ Often, when a song begins with a pickup measure, the missing beat(s) can be found in the song's final measure.

14

Technique Tips and Reminders

- As you work on the melodies played on the A string, be sure to arch your fingertips up and press the string with the tip of your finger. Don't lay them flat or they'll press against the E string as well. Later on, you'll need to make all the strings ring clearly, so get in the habit of playing with good technique now.

- Keep the mandolin up high, using a strap. Don't hunch over your instrument, and don't turn it upward to see the fretboard. Remember to play with your fingers, not your eyes!

- Keep your thumb behind the neck, as if your thumb and fingers are making a clamp to press the strings down.

Track 21

The Old Pickup

By the way, it's much better to practice a little every day than it is to cram everything into one long session; your fingers and your mind need time to develop. Whenever you practice, take a few minutes to warm up with some earlier lessons and songs, and then tackle the new stuff.

Track 22

Blue Dog in a Red Pickup

Lesson 4: The Third String: D

Track 23

For this string, we'll learn four new notes. Don't forget to check your tuning.

D

■ To play the note D, just pick the open 3rd string.

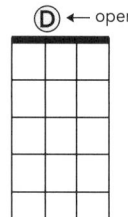

E

▶ Notice that the note E is on the second fret, just like the note B that we learned earlier.

■ For the next note, E, press your first finger on the 3rd string directly behind the second fret.

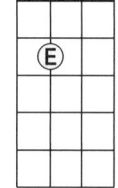

F

▶ Notice that the note F is on the third fret, just like the notes C (A string) and G (E string) that we learned earlier.

■ For the note F, press your second finger on the 3rd string directly behind the third fret.

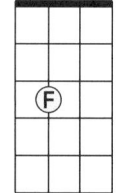

G

▶ Notice that the note G is on the fifth fret, just like the notes D (A string) and A (E string) that we learned earlier.

■ For the note G, press your fourth finger on the 3rd string directly behind the fifth fret.

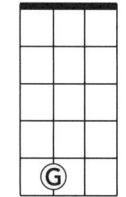
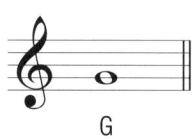

Track 24

D-String Jam

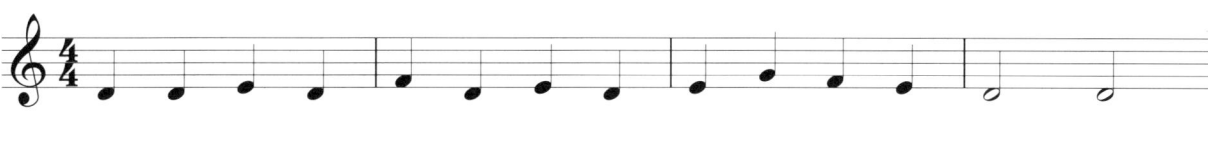

Track 25

Introducing Octaves

Congratulations! You've covered twelve different notes on your mandolin. Because the musical system uses only seven different note names (A–B–C–D–E–F–G), we need to recycle these names over and over to cover all the notes we hear. Whenever we use up all seven note names and need to use an eighth, we call the distance between the first and eighth notes an **octave** ("oct" comes from the Latin word for "eight," like "octopus" or "octagon").

You've already covered an octave between the open 2nd string (A) and the note at the 5th fret on the 1st string (also an A). Take a moment now to play these two notes at the same time. If your mandolin is in tune, you should hear that they sound very smooth together.

The next three songs all emphasize the distance of an octave. We've identified the octaves in "Double Down on the D." See if you can identify the octaves in "Octopus Ink" and "Real Gone Octagon."

Track 26

Double Down on the D

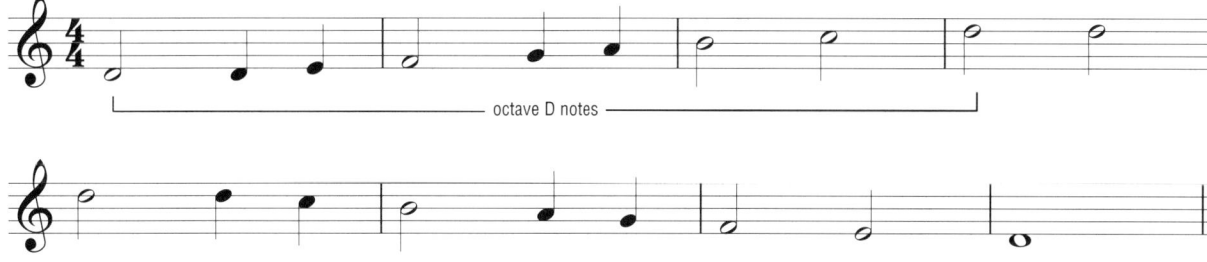

Track 27

Octopus Ink

▶ Watch out! There are a lot of jumps from the 3rd string to the 1st string in this one.

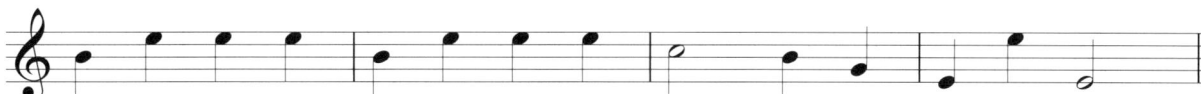

17

Real Gone Octagon

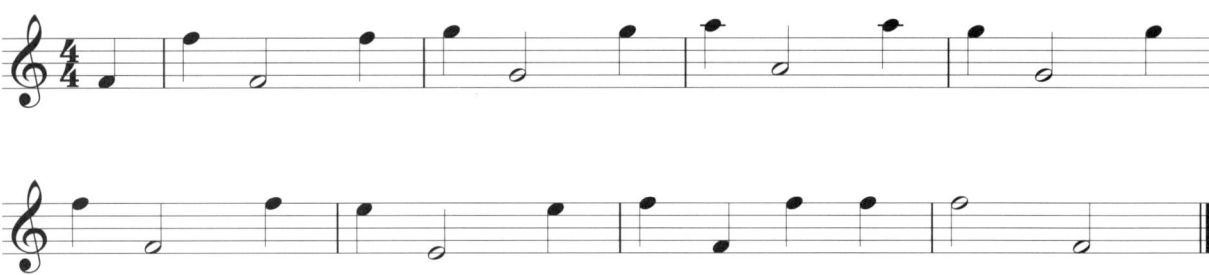

Sharps, Flats, and Naturals

In our naming of notes, you probably noticed that some frets have been named and some haven't. Perhaps you've been wondering about all the notes we've been skipping over. These notes will be named with new symbols called sharps and flats. Sharps, flats, and another symbol called a natural are musical symbols called **accidentals**, which raise or lower the pitch of a note:

A *sharp* (♯) raises the pitch of a note by one fret.

A *flat* (♭) lowers the pitch of a note by one fret.

A *natural* (♮) cancels a sharp or a flat, returning a note to its original pitch.

In musical terms, the distance of one fret is called a **half step**. When a song requires a note to be a half step higher or lower, you'll see a sharp (♯), flat (♭), or natural (♮) in front of it. This tells you to raise or lower the note for that measure only. Let's begin by learning one new note: F♯.

■ To play the note F♯, press your first finger on the 1st string directly behind the second fret.

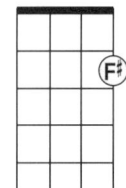

Try this short exercise with the new F♯ note.

Looking Sharp

▶ This song is in a 3/4 time signature, which indicates three beats per measure. For more on 3/4, see page 24.

18

Track 31

It's a Natural Fact

▶ Here's a chance to use both the new F♯ and your old friend, F, which can also be named F natural (♮). Try to play both the F natural and F♯ with your first finger.

Track 32

Surfin' Agent Sharp

Track 33

Finding Another F♯

You can be sure that if there's an F♯ located one fret higher than the F on the 1st string, there's an F♯ above the F on the 3rd string. Let's get back to the notes on the 3rd and 2nd strings and work on adding the F♯. Here's how to play it:

F♯

■ To play the note F♯ on the 3rd string, press your third finger directly behind the fourth fret.

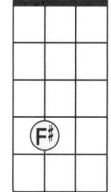

F♯

Hard-Time Blues

From D to Shining D

Lesson 5: The Fourth String: G

Track 36

Are you ready for the final, 4th string? Good! Just like the others, there are four natural notes to learn.

G

- To play the note G, just pick the open 4th string.

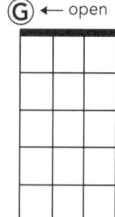

A

- To play the note A, press your first finger on the 4th string directly behind the second fret.

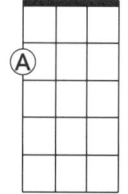

B

- To play the note B, press your third finger on the 4th string directly behind the fourth fret.

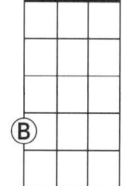
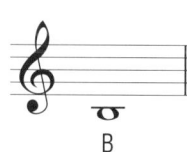

C

- To play the note C, press your fourth finger on the 4th string directly behind the fifth fret.

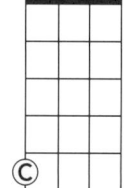

Track 37

Workout on G

Track 38

Four on the Floor

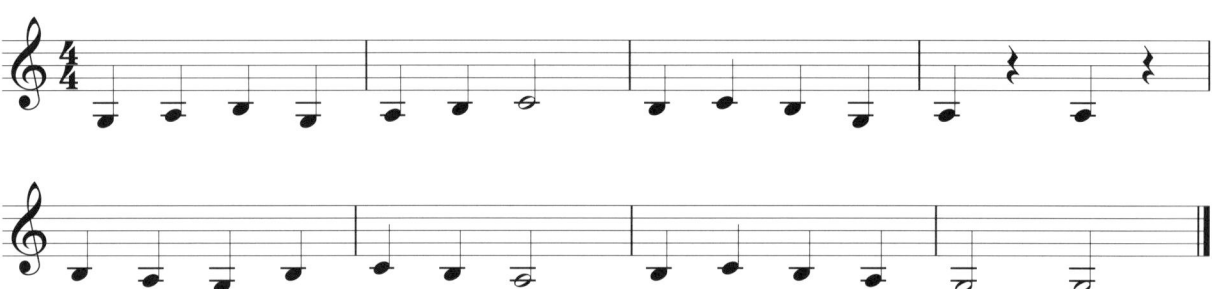

Track 39

Practicing with a Metronome

A *metronome* is a simple device that provides a steady beat or pulse to practice with. It is calibrated in beats per minute (abbreviated "bpm") and ranges from about 40 to 200 or more bpm. You'll find the most comfortable range between 60 and 180 bpm. Using a metronome is a great way to help your rhythmic ability, but it's not always the best way to begin to learn a piece of music. Instead of trying to play a piece quickly, take the time to know the notes individually. Play slowly and play every note with confidence. Then, try to find a slow, comfortable pulse on your metronome that matches the speed you've begun to practice at. Write down this speed next to the music, and try to increase it by 10–15 percent (two to three settings on most metronomes) whenever you practice until you can play at the speed you want.

Old Joe Clark

▶ You'll hear "Old Joe Clark" at three different metronome speeds. Can you keep in time with all three?

Sweet Blue Shuffle

Introducing Eighth Notes

So far, we've been reading rhythms with whole notes, whole rests, half notes, half rests, quarter notes, and quarter rests. When we divide a quarter note in half, we get two **eighth notes**. Two eighth notes take up as much time as one quarter note—usually one beat. When two eighth notes occur in one beat, they are connected with a beam. This makes them easier to read. Sometimes eighth notes are connected in groups of three or four, too.

When an eighth note occurs by itself, it has a flag tied to the end of its stem, like this:

Eighth notes are counted by adding the word "&" between each beat.

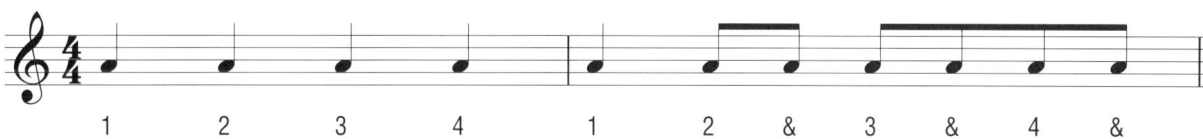

Eighth rests (𝄾) are counted just like eighth notes, except you stop the mandolin from ringing instead of playing.

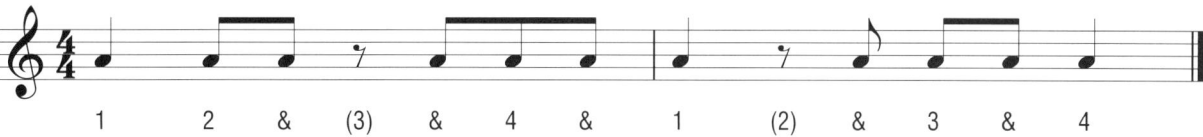

The numbers are called the **downbeats**, while the &s are called the **upbeats**.

Track 42

Eighth-Note Workout

► Practice these rhythms by tapping your foot, counting out loud, and clapping. Then try them on the mandolin. With only two different notes, you can focus on the rhythm!

Here are a couple of songs that put your eighth notes to use. Keep tapping your foot!

Track 43

Hot Cross Buns

Track 44

London Bridge

Track 45

3/4 Time

Although 4/4 is the most common time signature in music today, another common meter is **3/4**. In 3/4 time, there will be three beats to every measure. Quarter notes will still receive one beat each. Here's how to play and count all the different rhythms we've done in 3/4 time.

Here's a popular song in 3/4 time.

Track 46

Scarborough Fair

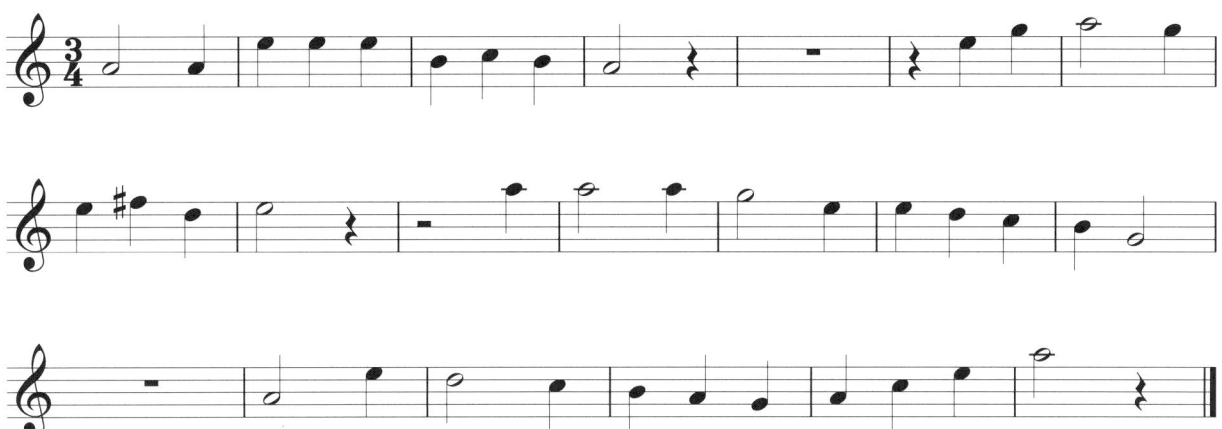

Track 47

New Notes: B♭ and C♯

It's time to add some new notes to our arsenal. First we're going to learn B♭. Remember the rule for finding flat notes: first find the natural note, then move down one fret. In the case of B♭, we'll find one on the 2nd string, first fret, and one on the 4th string, third fret.

B♭

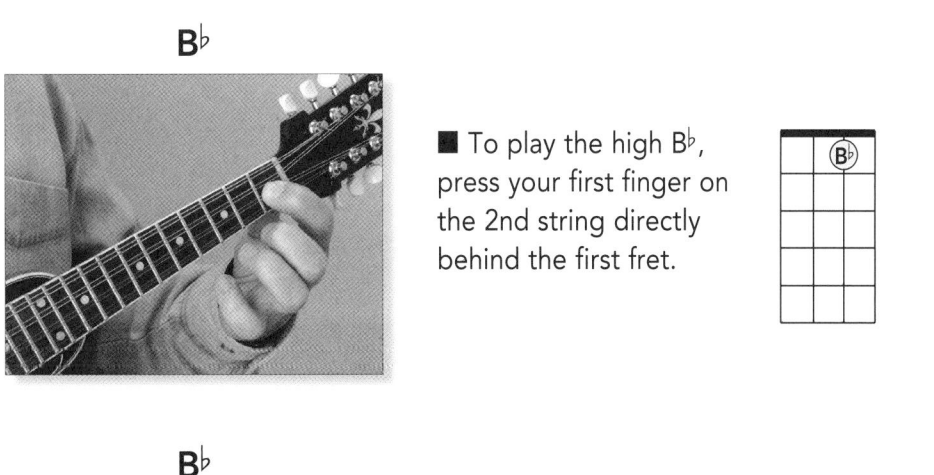

■ To play the high B♭, press your first finger on the 2nd string directly behind the first fret.

B♭

■ To play the low B♭, press your second finger on the 4th string directly behind the third fret.

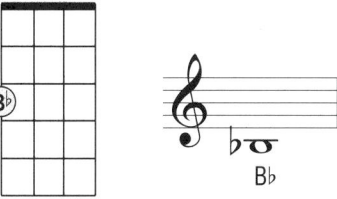

Here's another way of looking at it:

First play the note B on the 2nd string, then play the note one fret below it.

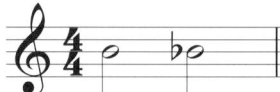

First play the note B on the 4th string, then play the note one fret below it.

Now let's try it with C♯. The rule for finding sharps is to first find the natural note, then find the note one fret higher.

C♯

■ To play the high C♯, press your third finger on the 2nd string directly behind the fourth fret.

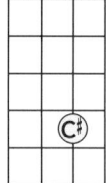 

C♯

■ To play the low C♯, press your fourth finger on the 4th string directly behind the sixth fret.

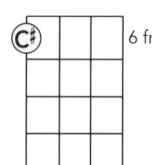 

Here's another way of looking at it:

First play the note C on the 2nd string, then play the note one fret above it.

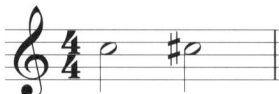

First play the note C on the 4th string, then play the note one fret above it.

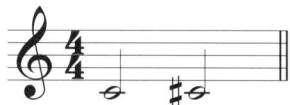

Here are two songs to put our new notes to work.

Track 48

Bourrée

Track 49

Mando Rock

Ties and Dots

The *tie* is a curved line that connects two notes of the same pitch. When you see a tie, play the first note and hold it for the total value of both notes.

Ties are useful when you need to extend the value of a note across a bar line. Another way to extend the value of a note is to use a *dot*. A dot extends any note by one-half its value. Most common is the dotted half note:

You'll encounter the dotted half note in many songs, especially those in 3/4 time.

Track 50

Greensleeves

Track 51

A Cabin in the Woods

Track 52

Square Knot

Track 53

Fall Back to Summer

Lesson 6 | **Chords**

Track 54

Now that you've got a handle on all four string courses, it's time to start learning about chords. *"What's a chord?"* you ask. A **chord** is three or more different notes played simultaneously. We'll start off with three common major chords. (More about what "major" means later.)

To play a chord, first get your left-hand fingers into position; the dots on each grid below tell you where to fret the string courses, and the numbers tell you what fingers to use. Then, with your right hand, strum downward across the strings. Our first chords will use just a couple of fingers along with a couple of open strings (indicated with an "O").

G

▶ Major chords are so common that we rarely bother to call them "major."

■ To play the G chord, press with your first and second fingers as shown, then strum downward across all four strings. Notice that your thumb will feel comfortable behind the neck when you play this chord.

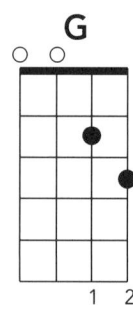

C

■ The C chord is a lot like the G chord. Press with your first and second fingers as shown, then strum downward across all four strings. Notice that your thumb will feel comfortable behind the neck when you play this chord.

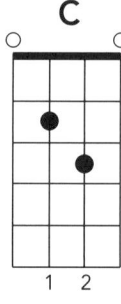

D

■ The D chord is a bit different. Be sure you have both fingers on the same fret, then strum downward across all four strings. Notice that your thumb will feel comfortable around the neck when you play this chord.

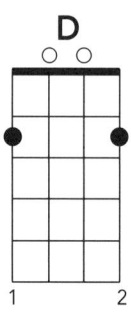

Troubleshooting Chords

If a chord sounds bad, try playing through it again, but slowly, one string course at a time. If you find a "problem note," readjust your finger or your hand position and try again. Be sure to arch your fingers and press with their tips. If you let your fingers fall flat, they will block other strings from ringing. And just as with single notes, you'll get the clearest tone by placing your fingertips as close to the frets as possible.

Introducing Tablature (Tab)

We'll be learning a new type of musical notation to go with chords called **tablature**, or "tab" for short. It consists of four lines—one for each string of your mandolin. The numbers written on the lines indicate which fret to play in order to sound the correct notes. Tab can be written alone or with standard music notation, as shown below.

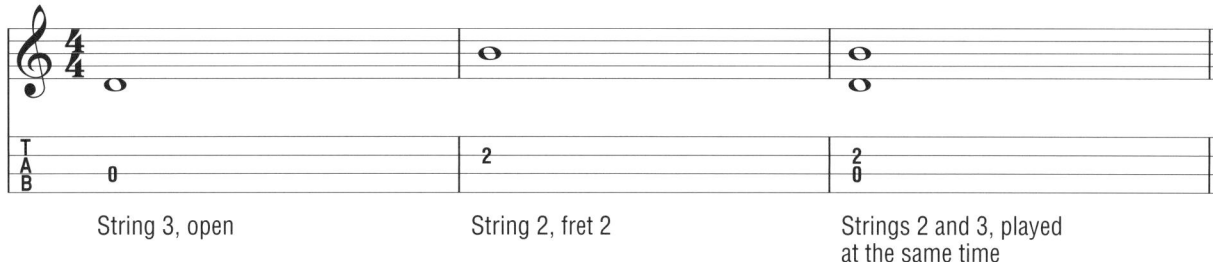

String 3, open   String 2, fret 2   Strings 2 and 3, played at the same time

Tab is a very popular notation method for mandolin music and can be used for melodies or chords.

Picking up the Tab

Track 55

▶ Here's a piece of music that uses standard notation, tab, and chord diagrams. You can use all three to learn the music better.

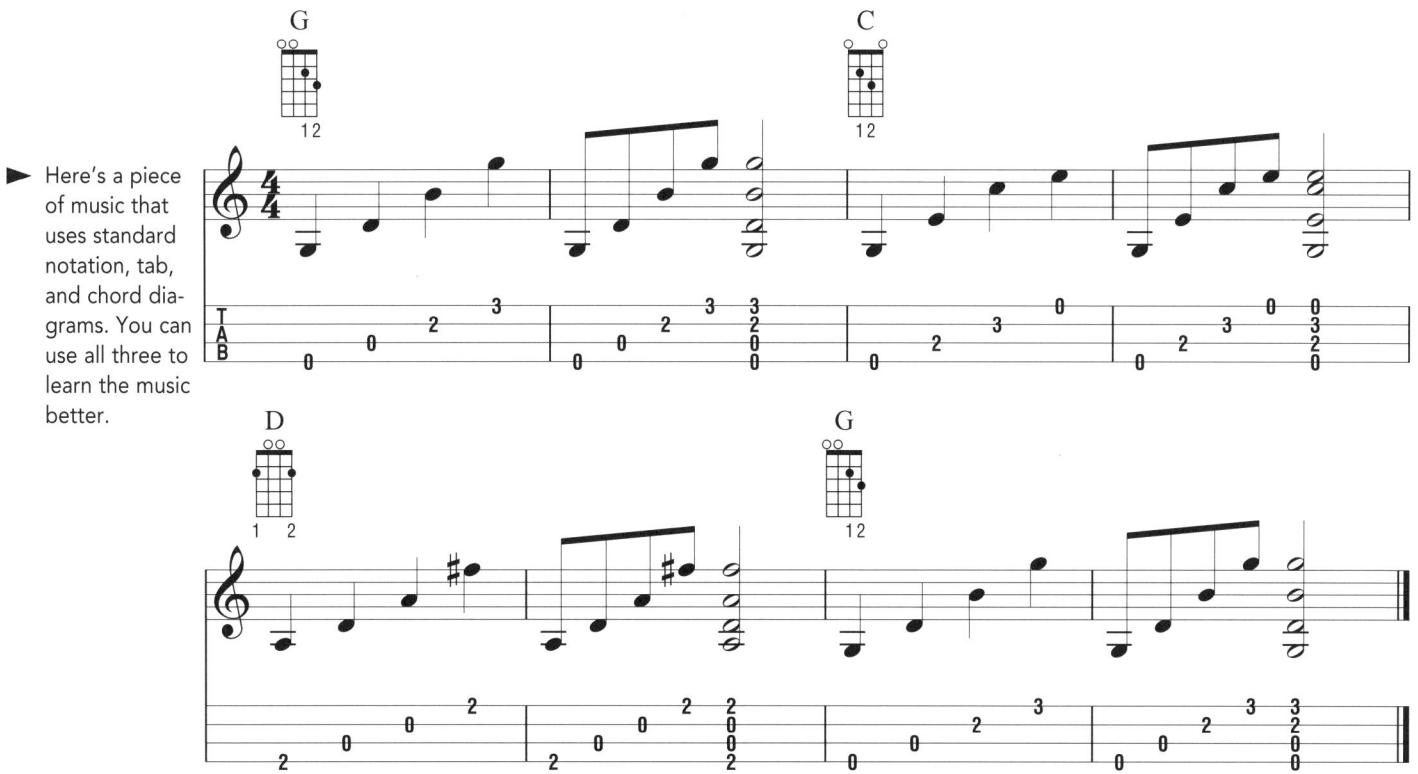

31

Track 56

A-Chord-Ingly

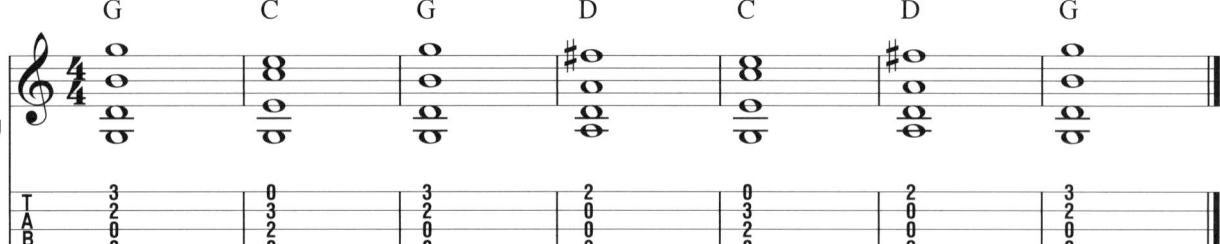

▶ See if you can play these chords by using just the music and tab.

Track 57

Chord-ially Yours

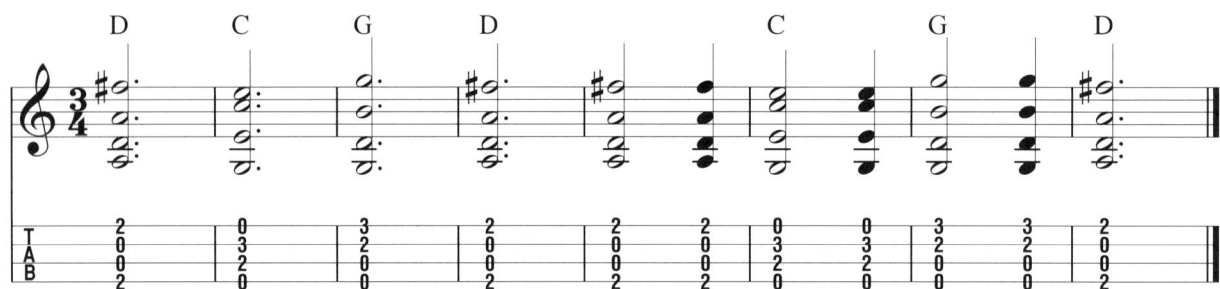

Track 58

Strumming Away

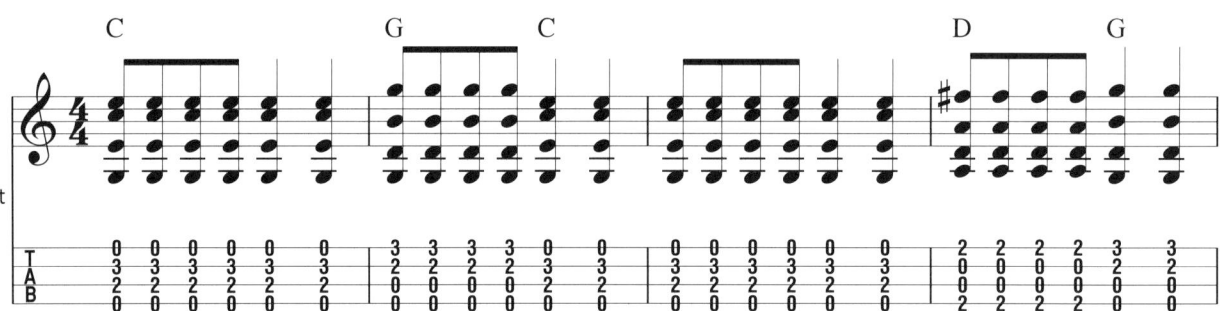

▶ The mandolin often strums chords as an accompaniment to the voice or other instruments.

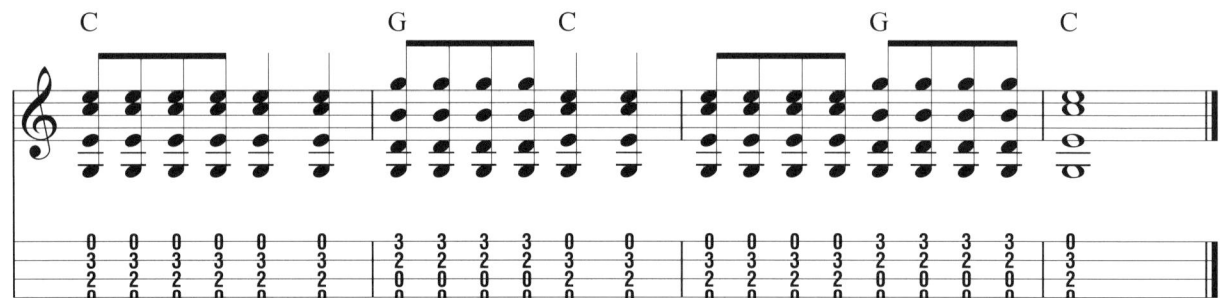

Track 59

Make a Note of It

▶ Sometimes we mix notes and chords, as in this piece.

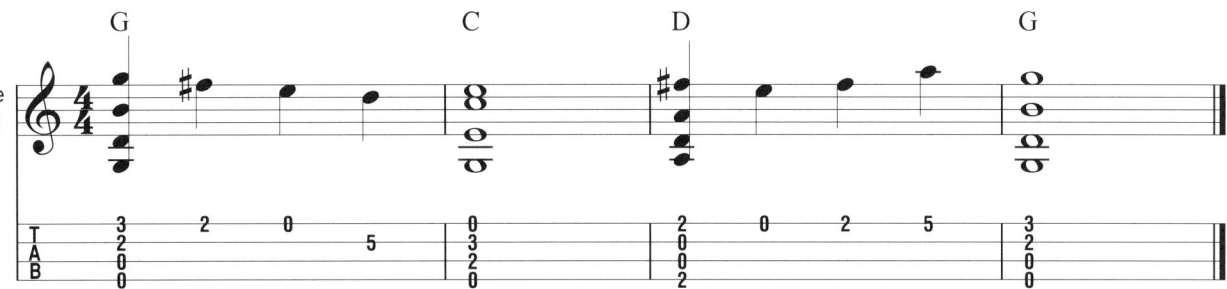

Track 60

Introducing Alternate Picking and Strumming

Alternate picking (also called "down/up picking") is an important technique for adding speed and accuracy to your mandolin playing. There are two parts to this pick stroke.

Picking or strumming the strings downward: This is how we've been playing all of our music so far. You should continue to use a downstroke for all notes that fall on a strong beat (the notes we count with numbers like "1," "2," "3," or "4"). Remember the downstroke symbol is "⊓."

Picking or strumming the strings upward: An upstroke is generally used for an eighth note that falls on the second half of the beat—the notes we count with the word "&." The upstroke symbol is "V."

Try the following exercises on each of your open strings using the alternate picking that the music indicates.

Picking Exercise #1

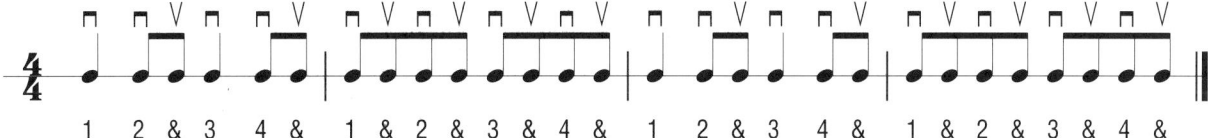

Picking Exercise #2

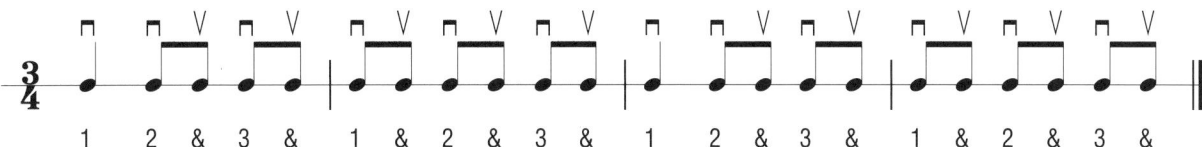

Rockin' 12-bar Blues

Track 61

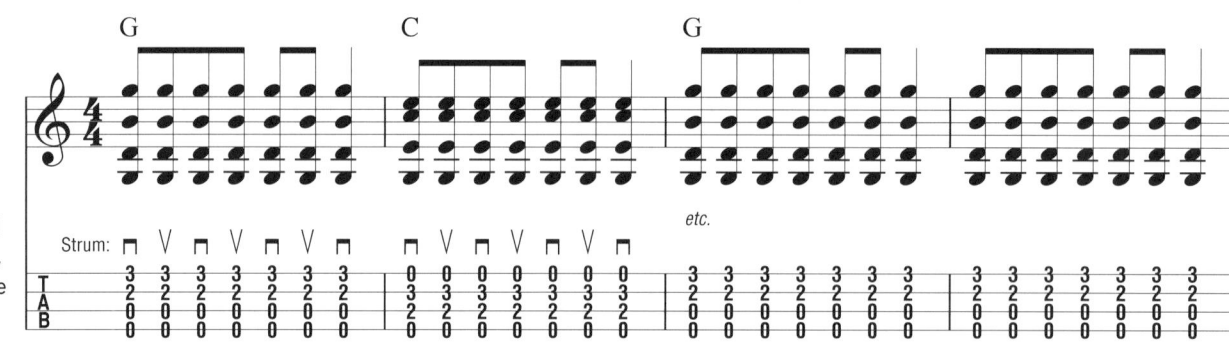
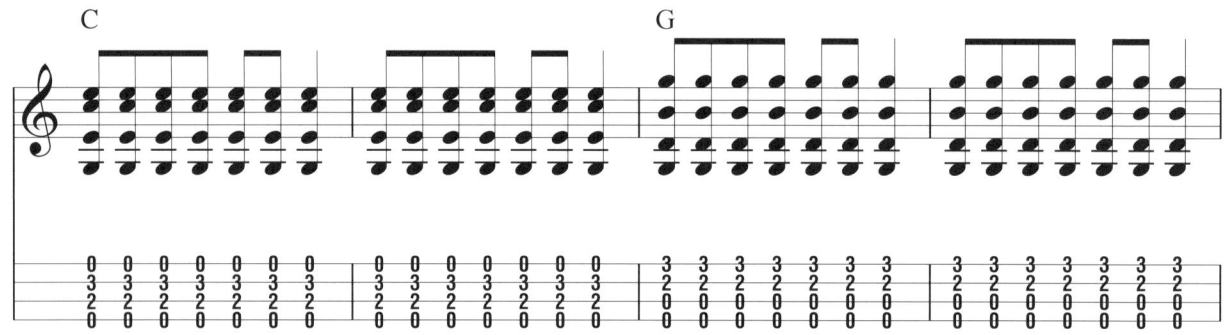
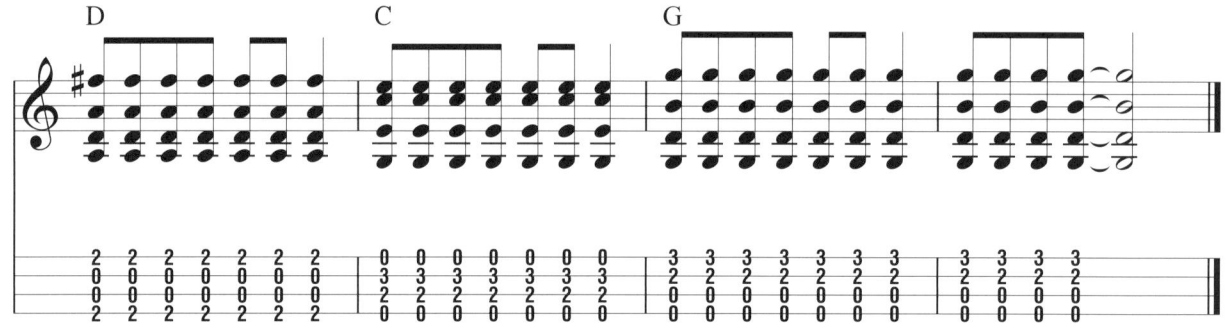

▶ The 12-bar blues is a common chord progression used in blues, rock, and jazz. Note that there are 12 bars, or measures. This should sound very familiar!

Track 62

Now that we've learned three major chords, let's tackle three *minor* chords. Notice that the minor chords are named with a small "m" after the chord name.

Dm

■ To play the Dm chord, press with your first and second fingers as shown, then strum across all four string courses.

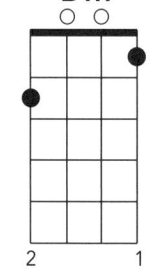
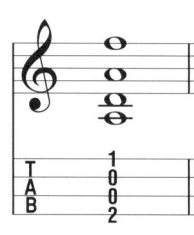

Am

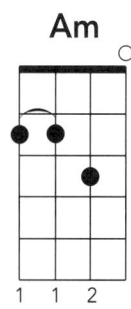
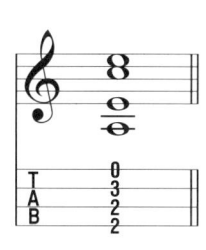

■ The Am chord is a tough one. Press down both the 3rd and 4th strings with the tip of the first finger (as shown by an arc connecting the dots in the diagram to the left), then add the second finger as shown. Be sure to arch the first finger up enough to let the open high E string ring.

Em

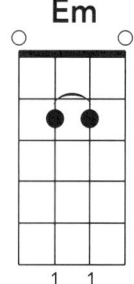
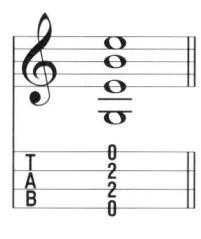

■ Like Am, the Em chord also requires one finger to cover two strings without touching the others.

Major and Minor—What's the Difference?

The difference between major and minor chords is in how they sound. Let's compare the D major chord and the D minor chord. The D major chord has a brighter sound, while the D minor is a little darker. You'll notice that just one note is different. Many people say that major chords have a happy or upbeat sound, while minor chords sound sad.

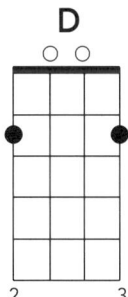
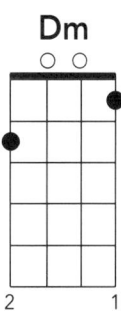

Remember when you read these chord names, major chords use just the letter name, while minor chords use the small "m" after the chord name. When we name these chords out loud, we often say just the letter name of the major chord, but we always say "minor" for the minor chords.

Ancient Voices

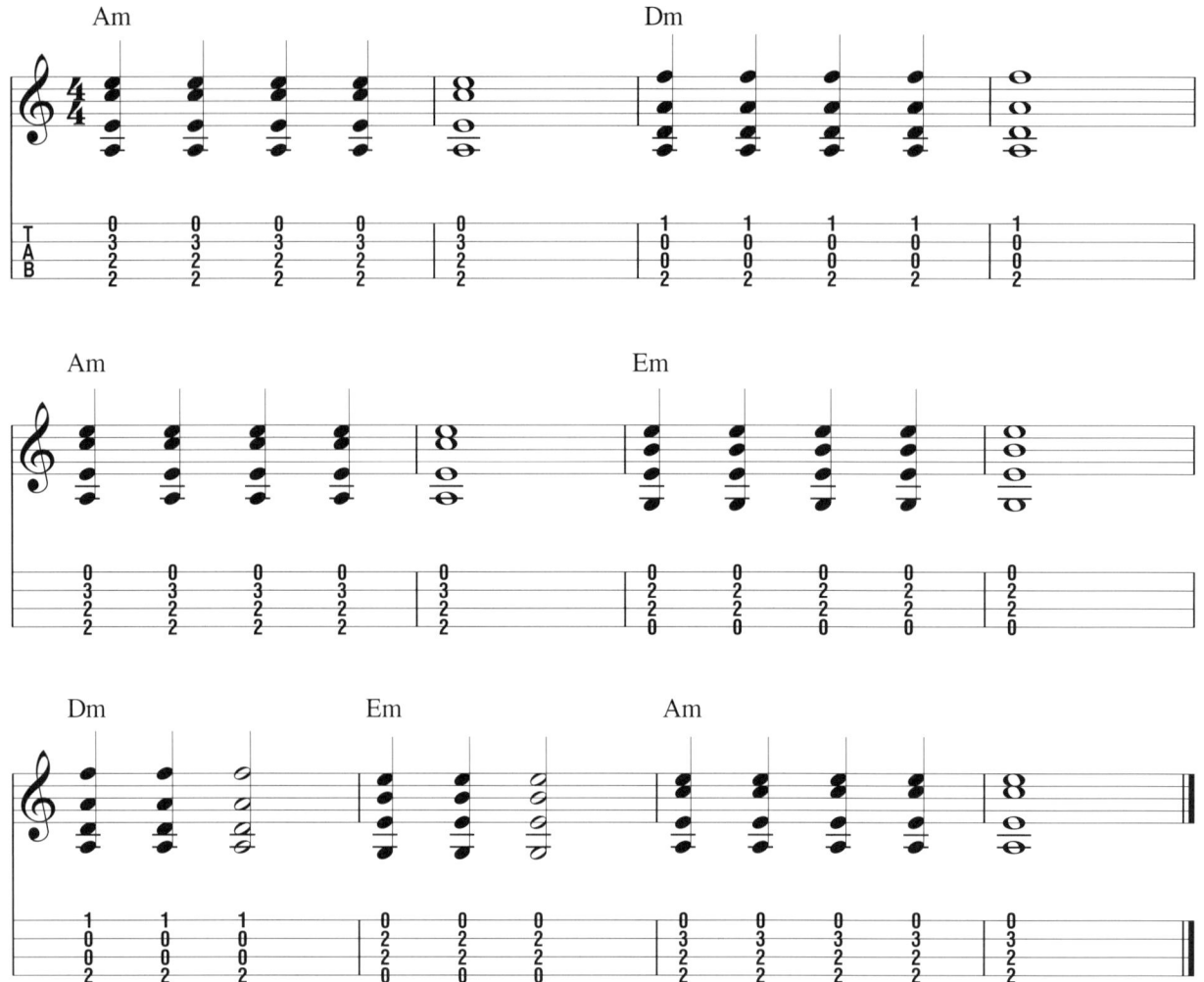

A Minor Miracle

Here's a chance to use your new minor chords with alternate strumming. Practice this a few times without your metronome, then try it at a slow speed, and finally try it at 92 bpm—the same speed as the audio track—*before* playing along with the audio.

Track 65

Cold Miner Blues

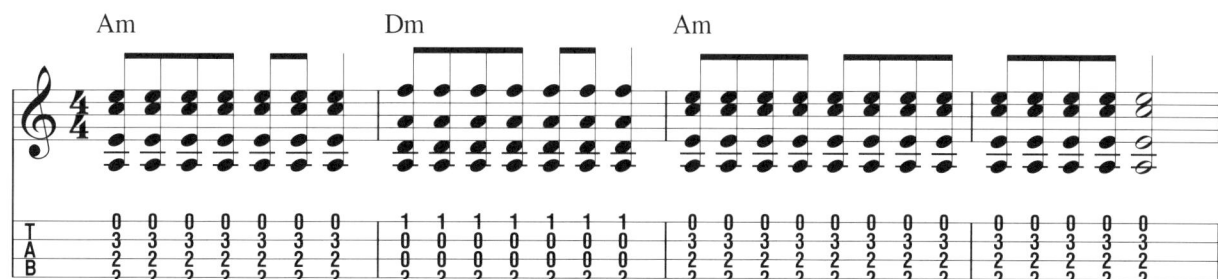

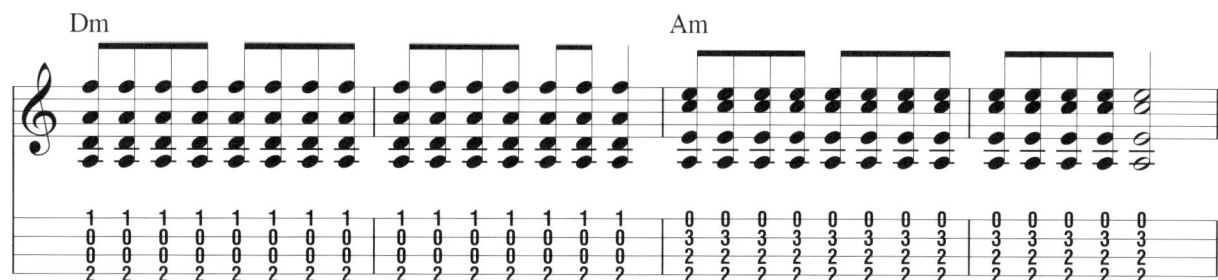

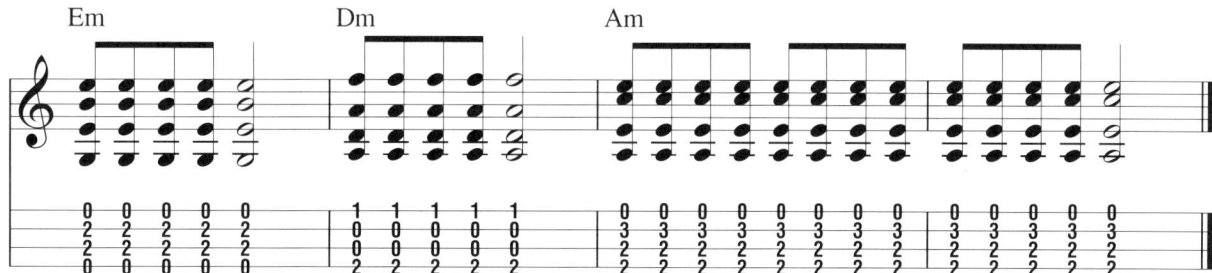

Lesson 7: The Major Scale

By now, you've probably noticed patterns of notes that have reappeared in many of the songs we've played. If you were to arrange these notes in a steadily rising or falling pattern, you would begin to create *scales*. Two things give a scale its name: its most important note (called the *root* or *tonic*, and usually the starting and ending note when we organize the scale) and the distance between the notes of the scale. The most common scale we've used so far is the major scale, and when it comes to naming notes, the easiest scale to understand is the C major scale. Here is a C major scale in one octave on the mandolin.

C Major Scale in One Octave

Track 66

▶ Remember that an octave is a distance of eight notes, as we learned in Lesson 4.

Notice that the C major scale uses no sharps or flats.

Now let's play an F major scale. Remember to reach to the first fret for the notes F and B♭.

F Major Scale in One Octave

Track 67

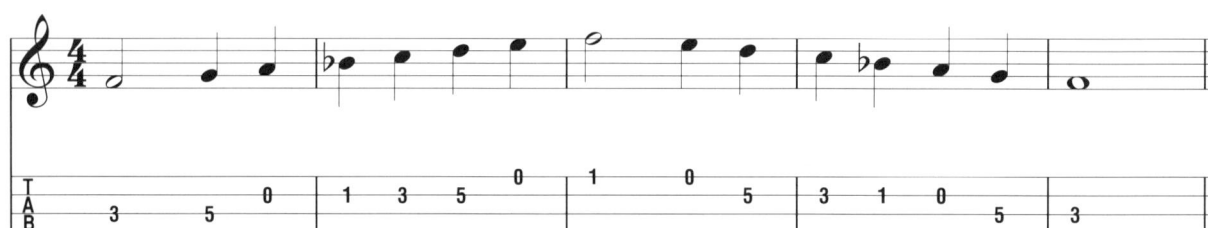

▶ Notice that the F major scale always uses one flat: B♭.

Now let's try a G major scale. Remember, we've already learned where the note G is in three different places: the open string, the note at the fifth fret of the 3rd string, and the note at the third fret of the 1st string. Because of this, we can play a G major scale in two octaves.

Track 68

G Major Scale in Two Octaves

▶ Notice that the G major scale always uses one sharp: F♯.

Scales, Keys, and Key Signatures

As we pointed out above, each of the different scales use different sets of notes.

    The C major scale uses the notes C–D–E–F–G–A–B.

    The F major scale uses the notes F–G–A–B♭–C–D–E.

    The G major scale uses the notes G–A–B–C–D–E–F♯.

When we use these sets of notes in their closest ascending and descending orders, with an even rhythm, and from one root to another an octave or two away, we call it a scale. When we use these sets of notes in any order at all, with lots of different rhythms, and without regard for staying within an exact octave, we call it a *key*. We usually show what key a piece of music is in by writing the appropriate sharps or flats at the beginning of the staff, between the clef and the time signature. This is called the *key signature*.

The key of C major has no sharps or flats.

Although there's just one B♭ shown, this will mean that every B will be flat.

Although there's just one F♯ shown, this will mean that every F will be sharp.

Sailing the C Major Sea

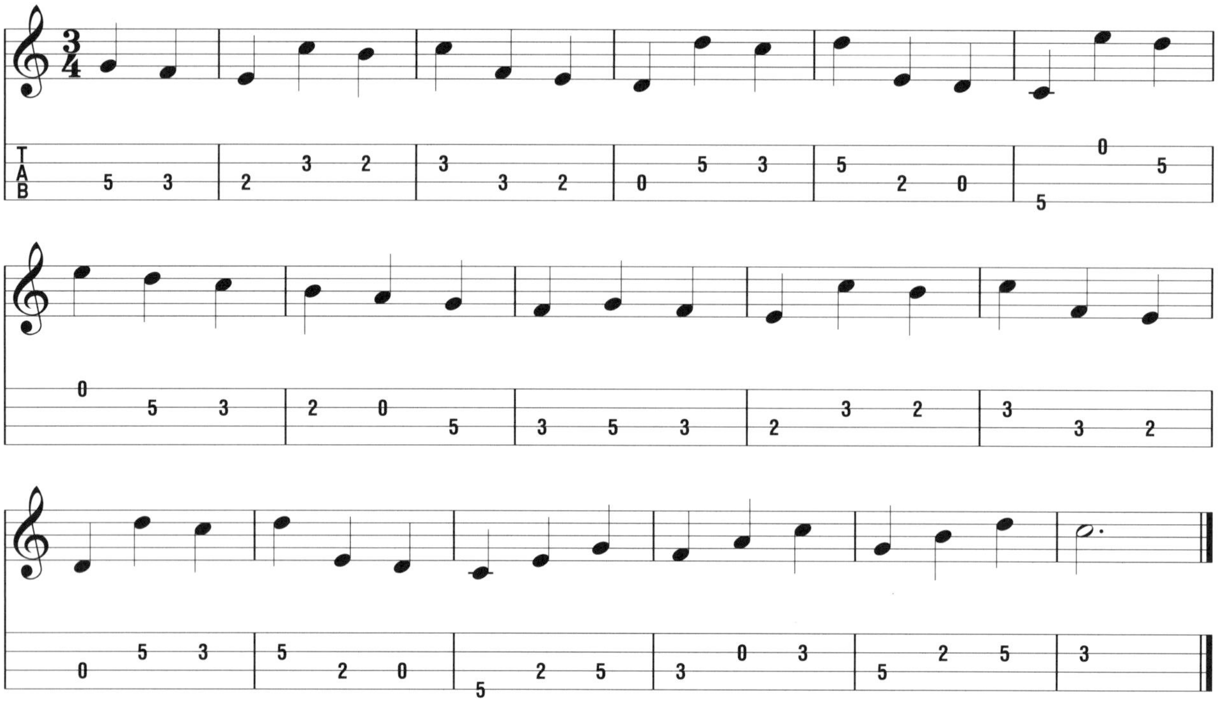

G-Zooey!

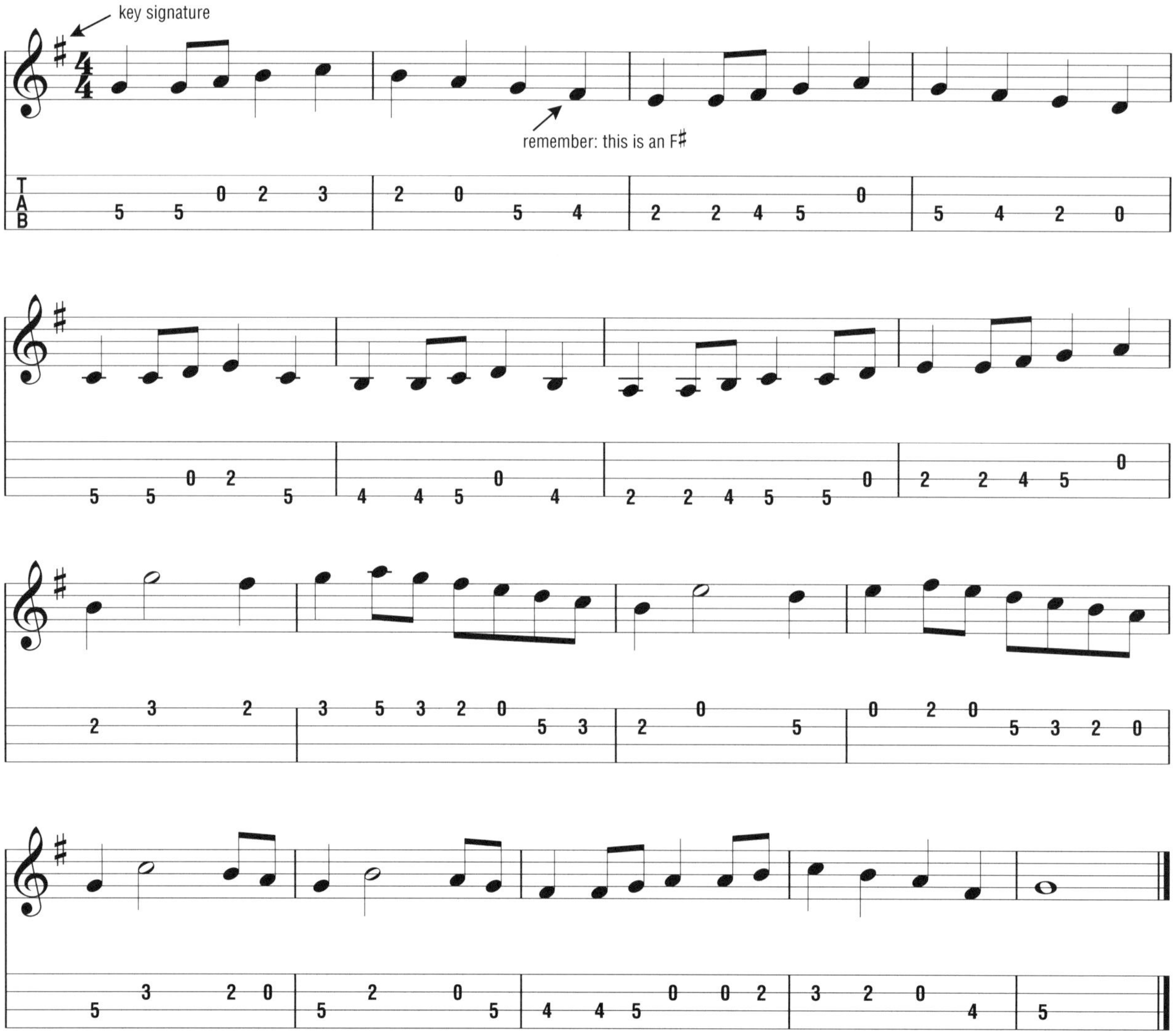

Track 71

F and Only F

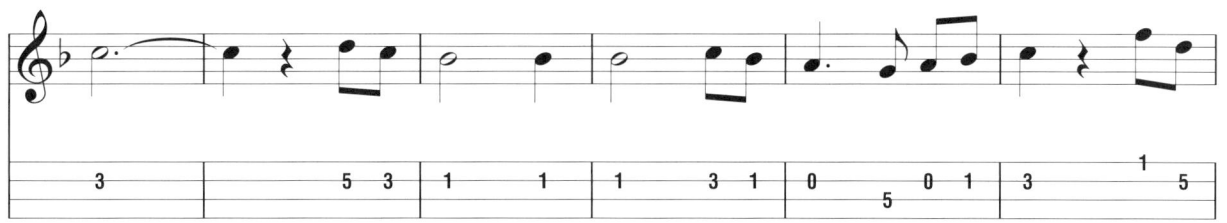

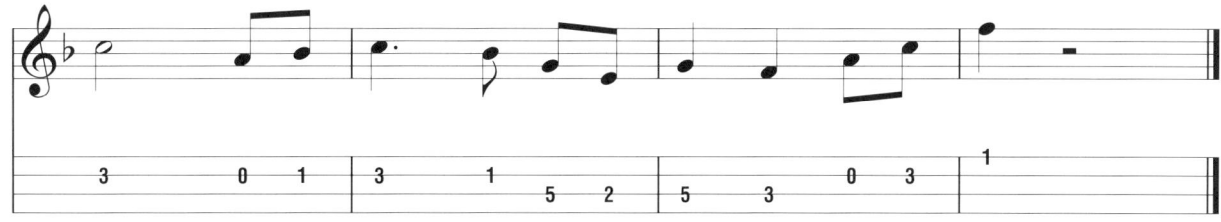

More Major Scales

Here are some more major scales. Scales are great for warming up. Notice that the key signatures contain either sharps or flats—but never both.

Track 72

D Major Scale in One Octave

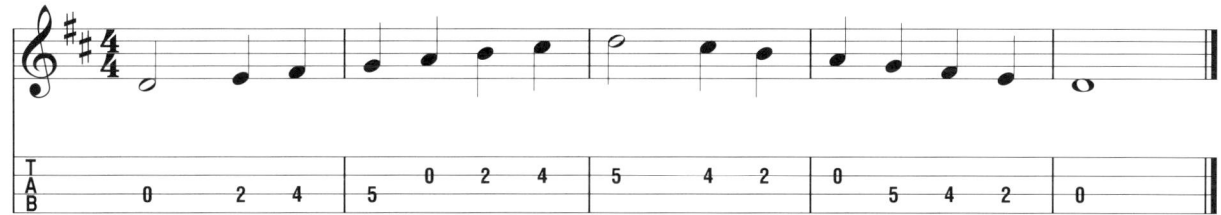

B♭ Major Scale in Two Octaves

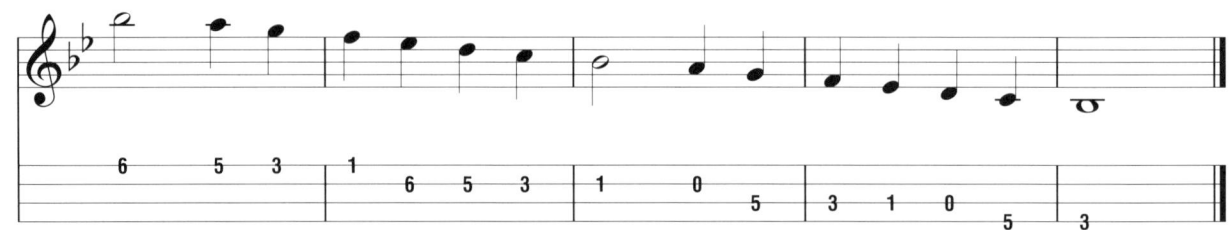

A Major Scale in Two Octaves

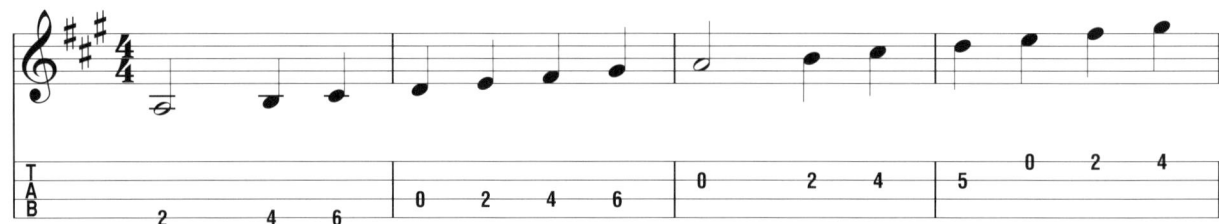

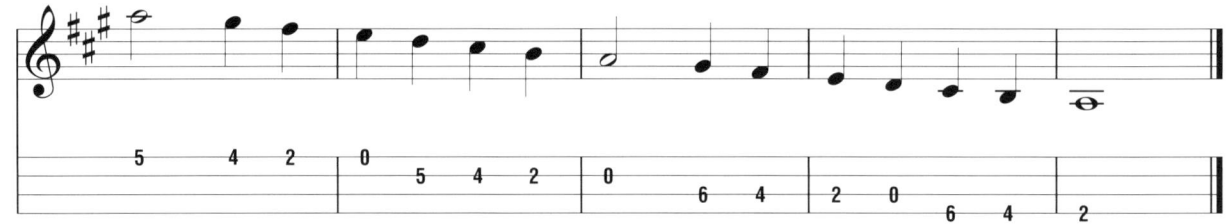

E Major Scale in One Octave

Lesson 8: Minor Scales & Movable Chords

Minor scales (and minor keys) have a much different sound than major scales and keys, but what's surprising is that those minor scales and keys are found *within* major scales and keys! Here's how it works:

Let's begin with the key of C major. You'll remember from the last chapter that the key of C major is made up of the notes C–D–E–F–G–A–B–C, and that the note C is the root or tonic. So what happens if we keep the notes of C major but start and end on some note besides C? We get a *mode* of the key of C major, that's what! We could start and end on D, for instance (D–E–F–G–A–B–C–D), or on E (E–F–G–A–B–C–D–E). Each of these modes has a different sort of musical personality. Besides the major scale itself, the mode that stands out the most is the one that starts on the sixth note of the major scale. In the key of C, that's the note A. The mode would read A–B–C–D–E–F–G–A, and we commonly call this the key of A minor.

Yes, the notes of C major are exactly the same as the notes of A minor. Let's play an A minor scale to see what it sounds like.

A Minor Scale in Two Octaves

Track 76

▶ Notice that the key of A minor has the same key signature as C major: no sharps or flats.

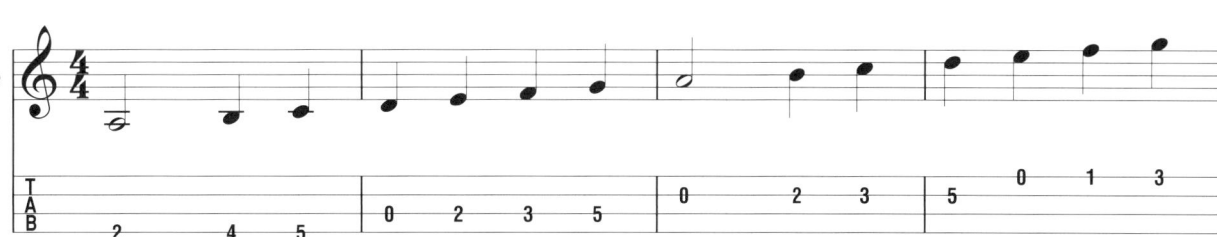

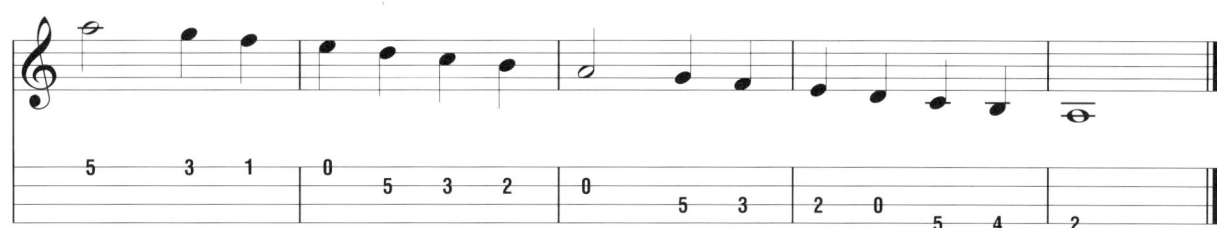

We often say the keys that share the same notes are *relative* to each other: The key of A minor is the *relative minor* of C major, and the key of C major is the *relative major* of A minor. If we look back at the major scales we played in the last chapter, we should be able to play a relative minor scale for every one of those major scales. Here are a couple more minor scales to get you started.

D Minor Scale in One Octave

Track 77

▶ D minor is the relative minor of F major. Both keys have the same key signature: one flat, B♭.

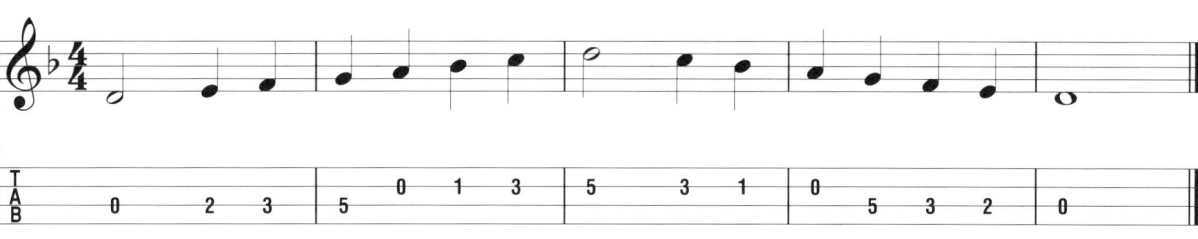

Track 78

E Minor Scale in One Octave

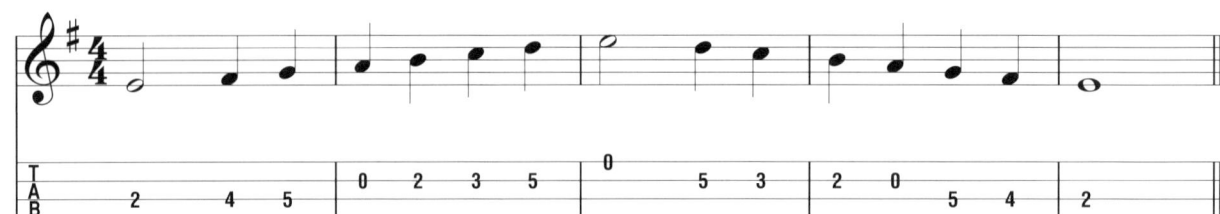

▶ E minor is the relative minor of G major. Both keys share the key signature of F♯.

Here are some songs in minor keys.

Track 79

When Johnny Comes Marching Home

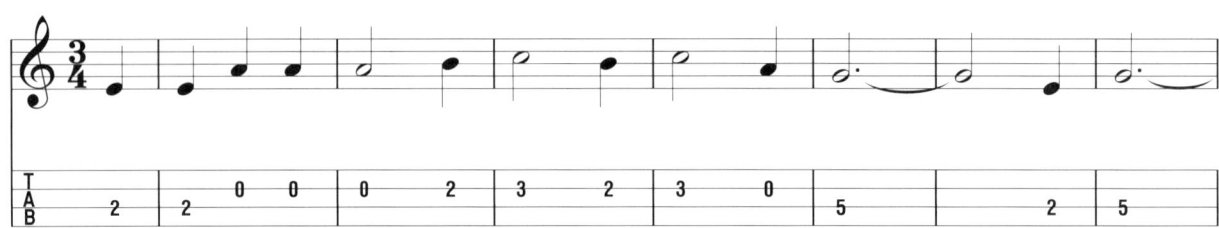

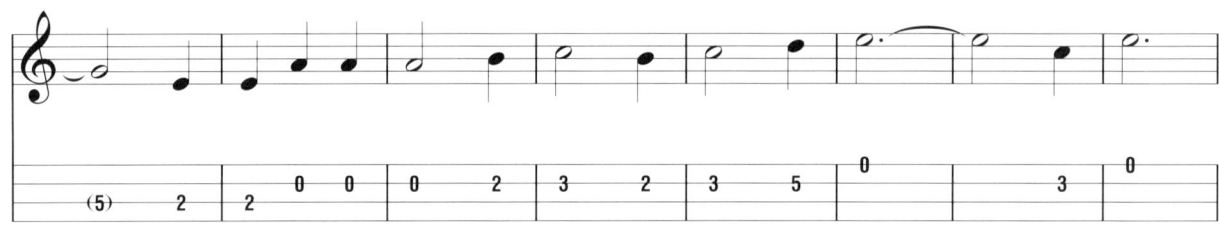

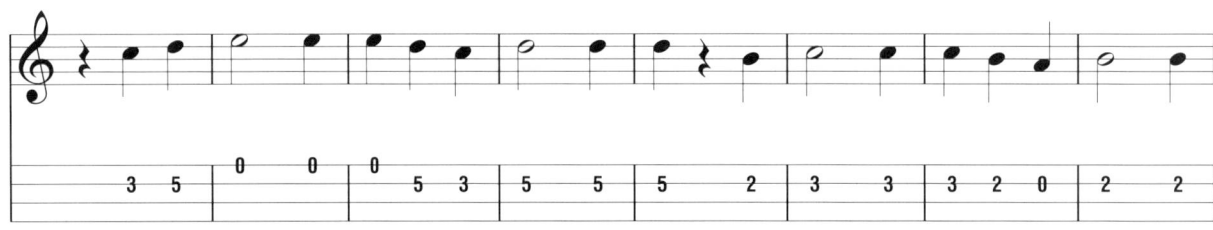

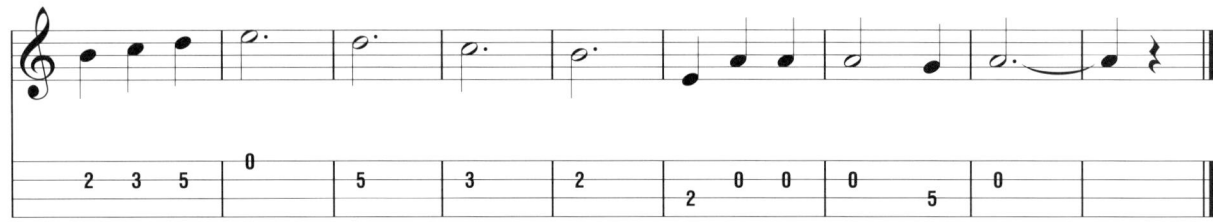

Broken Hearts

Introducing Movable Chords

Remember the chords we learned back in Chapter 6? Those chords are often called **open chords** because they are played with open strings. If you move your fingers up or down a fret while keeping the open strings open, you will get some chords that are very different from what you started with. You might get some interesting sounding chords and some terrible-sounding chords, but they will certainly sound much different than the chord you started with, and they will have some musically-complicated names.

For example, play a D chord, then move your fingers up one fret, as shown below:

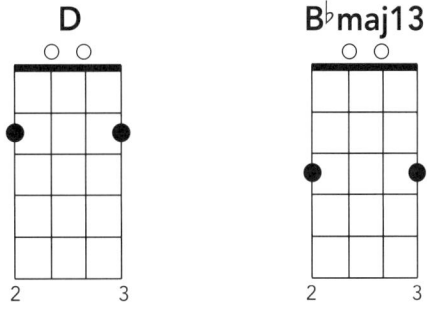

The resulting chord, B♭maj13, is nothing like a D major chord.

Now it's time to learn a new kind of chord fingering called a movable chord. In a **movable chord**, the fingers cover all four strings. If you move your fingers up or down a fret, the chord has the same quality (usually major or minor) and sounds very similar.

Here is the fingering for an A major chord with a movable fingering.

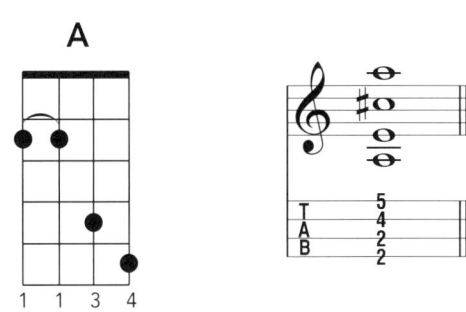

45

If we move this shape up two frets, it becomes a B major chord. It remains a simple major chord, but with a different root or tonic note.

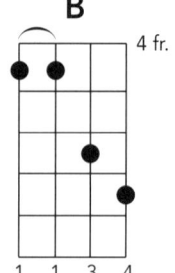

Another useful feature of this fingering is that we need to change only one note in the shape to make it a minor chord.

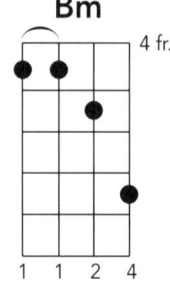
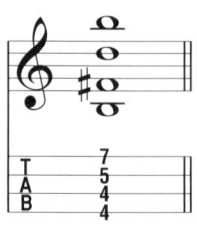

This next piece of music uses the movable chord shapes that we just learned (Bm, A, and B major) as well as an open G chord. It's in a minor key, too—can you figure out what minor key it's in?

The Lonely Mandolin

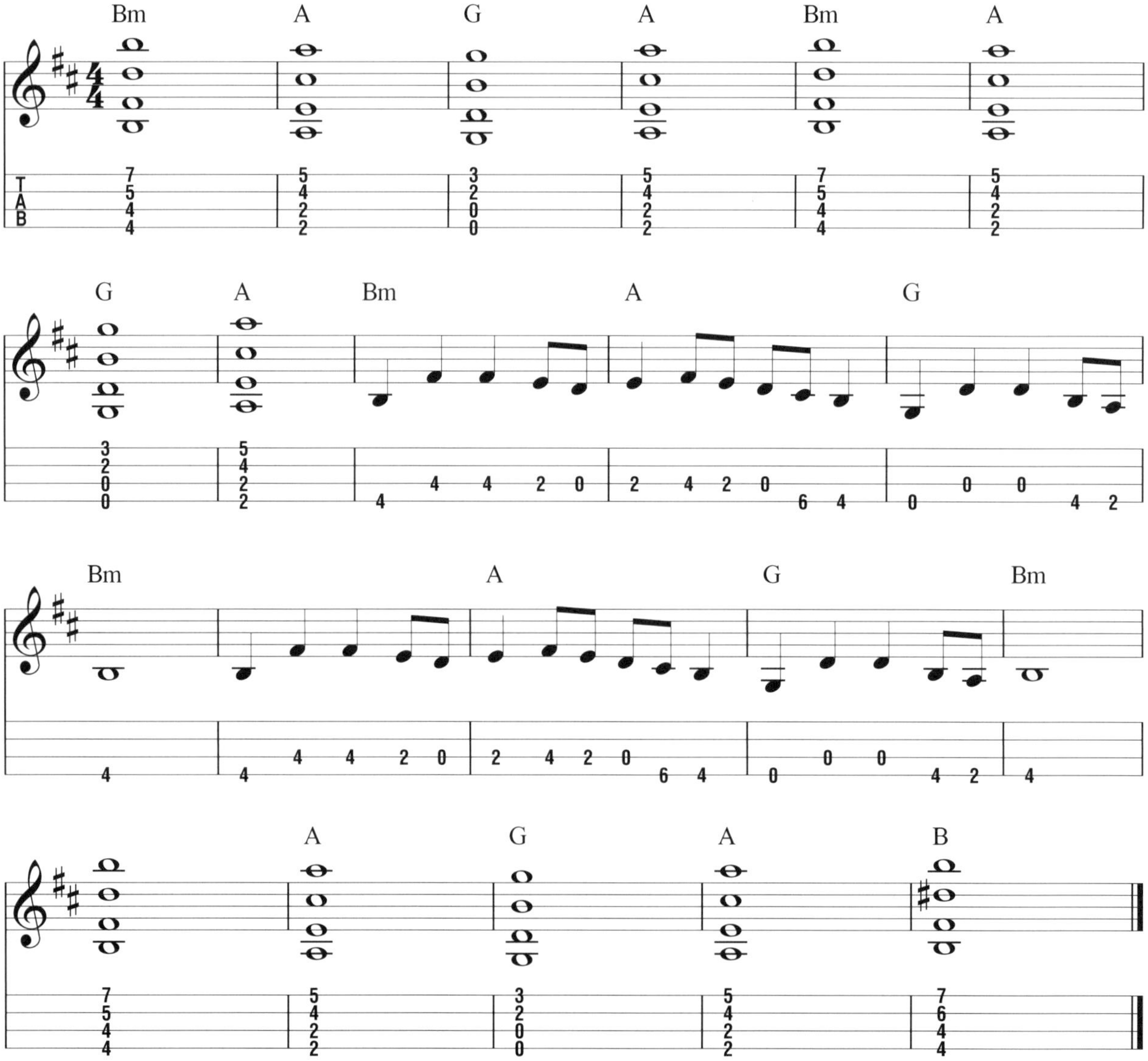

Track 83

More Movable Chords

Did you notice that the A major and B major chords you just learned had a shape much like the open G major chord? Let's now use the shape of the open D major chord to learn some more movable chords.

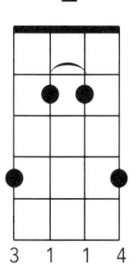
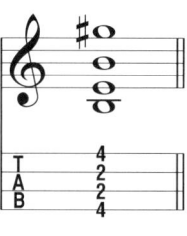

Here is an E major chord with a movable fingering.

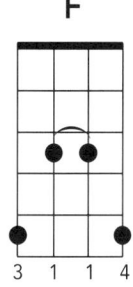
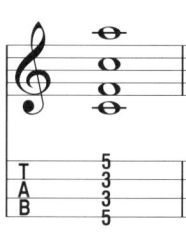

If we move this shape up one fret, it becomes an F major chord. It remains a simple major chord, but with a different root or tonic note.

Another useful feature of this fingering is that we need to change only one note in the shape to make it a minor chord.

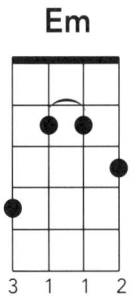
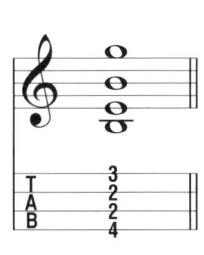
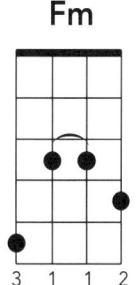
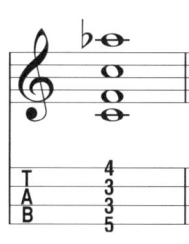

Track 84

Moving Day

Track 85

Back and Forth

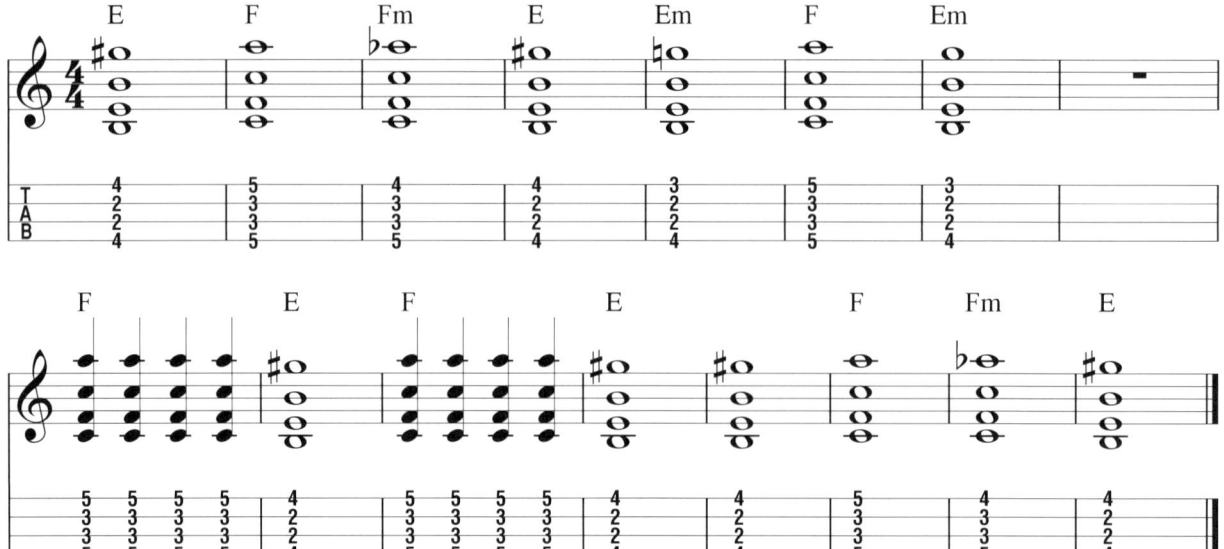

Track 86

Aura Lee

On this track, you can play either the chords or the melody, but notice that only the chord names are given. There are neither grid diagrams nor tablature shown for the chords. Try to memorize the shapes and play it both ways.